THE LIFE AND DEATH OF KING RICHARD II

WILLIAM SHAKESPEARE

Actus Primus

Scena Prima.

Enter King Richard, Iohn of Gaunt, with other Nobles and Attendants.

King Richard. Old Iohn of Gaunt, time-honoured Lancaster,

Hast thou according to thy oath and band

Brought hither Henry Herford thy bold son:

Heere to make good y boistrous late appeale,

Which then our leysure would not let vs heare,

Against the Duke of Norfolke, Thomas Mowbray?

Gaunt. I haue my Liege

King. Tell me moreouer, hast thou sounded him,

If he appeale the Duke on ancient malice,

Or worthily as a good subiect should

On some knowne ground of treacherie in him

Gaunt. As neere as I could sift him on that argument,

On some apparant danger seene in him,

Aym'd at your Highnesse, no inueterate malice

Kin. Then call them to our presence face to face,

And frowning brow to brow, our selues will heare

Th' accuser, and the accused, freely speake;

High stomack'd are they both, and full of ire,

In rage, deafe as the sea; hastie as fire.

Enter Bullingbrooke and Mowbray.

Bul. Many yeares of happy dayes befall

My gracious Soueraigne, my most louing Liege

Mow. Each day still better others happinesse,

Vntill the heauens enuying earths good hap,

Adde an immortall title to your Crowne

King. We thanke you both, yet one but flatters vs,

As well appeareth by the cause you come,

Namely, to appeale each other of high treason.

Coosin of Hereford, what dost thou obiect

Against the Duke of Norfolke, Thomas Mowbray?

Bul. First, heauen be the record to my speech,

In the deuotion of a subiects loue,

Tendering the precious safetie of my Prince,

And free from other misbegotten hate,

Come I appealant to this Princely presence.

Now Thomas Mowbray do I turne to thee,
And marke my greeting well: for what I speake,
My body shall make good vpon this earth,
Or my diuine soule answer it in heauen.
Thou art a Traitor, and a Miscreant;
Too good to be so, and too bad to liue,
Since the more faire and christall is the skie,
The vglier seeme the cloudes that in it flye:
Once more, the more to aggrauate the note,
With a foule Traitors name stuffe I thy throte,
And wish (so please my Soueraigne) ere I moue,
What my tong speaks, my right drawn sword may proue
Mow. Let not my cold words heere accuse my zeale:
'Tis not the triall of a Womans warre,
The bitter clamour of two eager tongues,
Can arbitrate this cause betwixt vs twaine:
The blood is hot that must be cool'd for this.
Yet can I not of such tame patience boast,
As to be husht, and nought at all to say.
First the faire reuerence of your Highnesse curbes mee,
From giuing reines and spurres to my free speech,
Which else would post, vntill it had return'd
These tearmes of treason, doubly downe his throat.
Setting aside his high bloods royalty,
And let him be no Kinsman to my Liege,
I do defie him, and I spit at him,
Call him a slanderous Coward, and a Villaine:

Which to maintaine, I would allow him oddes,

And meete him, were I tide to runne afoote,

Euen to the frozen ridges of the Alpes,

Or any other ground inhabitable,

Where euer Englishman durst set his foote.

Meane time, let this defend my loyaltie,

By all my hopes most falsely doth he lie

Bul. Pale trembling Coward, there I throw my gage,

Disclaiming heere the kindred of a King,

And lay aside my high bloods Royalty,

Which feare, not reuerence makes thee to except.

If guilty dread hath left thee so much strength,

As to take vp mine Honors pawne, then stoope.

By that, and all the rites of Knight-hood else,

Will I make good against thee arme to arme,

What I haue spoken, or thou canst deuise

Mow. I take it vp, and by that sword I sweare,

Which gently laid my Knight-hood on my shoulder,

Ile answer thee in any faire degree,

Or Chiualrous designe of knightly triall:

And when I mount, aliue may I not light,

If I be Traitor, or vniustly fight

King. What doth our Cosin lay to Mowbraies charge?

It must be great that can inherite vs,

So much as of a thought of ill in him

Bul. Looke what I said, my life shall proue it true,

That Mowbray hath receiu'd eight thousand Nobles,

In name of lendings for your Highnesse Soldiers,

The which he hath detain'd for lewd employments,

Like a false Traitor, and iniurious Villaine.

Besides I say, and will in battaile proue,

Or heere, or elsewhere to the furthest Verge

That euer was suruey'd by English eye,

That all the Treasons for these eighteene yeeres

Complotted, and contriued in this Land,

Fetch'd from false Mowbray their first head and spring.

Further I say, and further will maintaine

Vpon his bad life, to make all this good.

That he did plot the Duke of Glousters death,

Suggest his soone beleeuing aduersaries,

And consequently, like a Traitor Coward,

Sluc'd out his innocent soule through streames of blood:

Which blood, like sacrificing Abels cries,

(Euen from the toonglesse cauernes of the earth)

To me for iustice, and rough chasticement:

And by the glorious worth of my discent,

This arme shall do it, or this life be spent

King. How high a pitch his resolution soares:

Thomas of Norfolke, what sayest thou to this?

Mow. Oh let my Soueraigne turne away his face,

And bid his eares a little while be deafe,

Till I haue told this slander of his blood,

How God, and good men, hate so foule a lyar

King. Mowbray, impartiall are our eyes and eares,

Were he my brother, nay our kingdomes heyre,

As he is but my fathers brothers sonne;

Now by my Scepters awe, I make a vow,

Such neighbour-neerenesse to our sacred blood,

Should nothing priuiledge him, nor partialize

The vn-stooping firmenesse of my vpright soule.

He is our subiect (Mowbray) so art thou,

Free speech, and fearelesse, I to thee allow

Mow. Then Bullingbrooke, as low as to thy heart,

Through the false passage of thy throat; thou lyest:

Three parts of that receipt I had for Callice,

Disburst I to his Highnesse souldiers;

The other part reseru'd I by consent,

For that my Soueraigne Liege was in my debt,

Vpon remainder of a deere Accompt,

Since last I went to France to fetch his Queene:

Now swallow downe that Lye. For Glousters death,

I slew him not; but (to mine owne disgrace)

Neglected my sworne duty in that case:

For you my noble Lord of Lancaster,

The honourable Father to my foe,

Once I did lay an ambush for your life,

A trespasse that doth vex my greeued soule:

But ere I last receiu'd the Sacrament,

I did confesse it, and exactly begg'd

Your Graces pardon, and I hope I had it.

This is my fault: as for the rest appeal'd,

It issues from the rancour of a Villaine,

A recreant, and most degenerate Traitor,

Which in my selfe I boldly will defend,

And interchangeably hurle downe my gage

Vpon this ouer-weening Traitors foote,

To proue my selfe a loyall Gentleman,

Euen in the best blood chamber'd in his bosome.

In hast whereof, most heartily I pray

Your Highnesse to assigne our Triall day

King. Wrath-kindled Gentlemen be rul'd by me:

Let's purge this choller without letting blood:

This we prescribe, though no Physition,

Deepe malice makes too deepe incision.

Forget, forgiue, conclude, and be agreed,

Our Doctors say, This is no time to bleed.

Good Vnckle, let this end where it begun,

Wee'l calme the Duke of Norfolke; you, your son

Gaunt. To be a make-peace shall become my age,

Throw downe (my sonne) the Duke of Norfolkes gage

King. And Norfolke, throw downe his

Gaunt. When Harrie when? Obedience bids,

Obedience bids I should not bid agen

King. Norfolke, throw downe, we bidde; there is no boote

Mow. My selfe I throw (dread Soueraigne) at thy foot.

My life thou shalt command, but not my shame,

The one my dutie owes, but my faire name

Despight of death, that liues vpon my graue

To darke dishonours vse, thou shalt not haue.

I am disgrac'd, impeach'd, and baffel'd heere,

Pierc'd to the soule with slanders venom'd speare:

The which no balme can cure, but his heart blood

Which breath'd this poyson

King. Rage must be withstood:

Giue me his gage: Lyons make Leopards tame

Mo. Yea, but not change his spots: take but my shame,

And I resigne my gage. My deere, deere Lord,

The purest treasure mortall times afford

Is spotlesse reputation: that away,

Men are but gilded loame, or painted clay.

A Iewell in a ten times barr'd vp Chest,

Is a bold spirit, in a loyall brest.

Mine Honor is my life; both grow in one:

Take Honor from me, and my life is done.

Then (deere my Liege) mine Honor let me trie,

In that I liue; and for that will I die

King. Coosin, throw downe your gage,

Do you begin

Bul. Oh heauen defend my soule from such foule sin.

Shall I seeme Crest-falne in my fathers sight,

Or with pale beggar-feare impeach my hight

Before this out-dar'd dastard? Ere my toong,

Shall wound mine honor with such feeble wrong;

Or sound so base a parle: my teeth shall teare

The slauish motiue of recanting feare,

And spit it bleeding in his high disgrace,

Where shame doth harbour, euen in Mowbrayes face.

Exit Gaunt.

King. We were not borne to sue, but to command,

Which since we cannot do to make you friends,

Be readie, (as your liues shall answer it)

At Couentree, vpon S[aint]. Lamberts day:

There shall your swords and Lances arbitrate

The swelling difference of your setled hate:

Since we cannot attone you, you shall see

Iustice designe the Victors Chiualrie.

Lord Marshall, command our Officers at Armes,

Be readie to direct these home Alarmes.

Exeunt.

Scena Secunda.

Enter Gaunt, and Dutchesse of Gloucester.

Gaunt. Alas, the part I had in Glousters blood,

Doth more solicite me then your exclaimes,

To stirre against the Butchers of his life.

But since correction lyeth in those hands

Which made the fault that we cannot correct,

Put we our quarrell to the will of heauen,

Who when they see the houres ripe on earth,

Will raigne hot vengeance on offenders heads

Dut. Findes brotherhood in thee no sharper spurre?

Hath loue in thy old blood no liuing fire?

Edwards seuen sonnes (whereof thy selfe art one)

Were as seuen violles of his Sacred blood,

Or seuen faire branches springing from one roote:

Some of those seuen are dride by natures course,

Some of those branches by the destinies cut:

But Thomas, my deere Lord, my life, my Glouster,

One Violl full of Edwards Sacred blood,

One flourishing branch of his most Royall roote

Is crack'd, and all the precious liquor spilt;

Is hackt downe, and his summer leafes all vaded

By Enuies hand, and Murders bloody Axe.

Ah Gaunt! His blood was thine, that bed, that wombe,

That mettle, that selfe-mould that fashion'd thee,

Made him a man: and though thou liu'st, and breath'st,

Yet art thou slaine in him: thou dost consent

In some large measure to thy Fathers death,

In that thou seest thy wretched brother dye,

Who was the modell of thy Fathers life.

Call it not patience (Gaunt) it is dispaire,

In suffring thus thy brother to be slaughter'd,

Thou shew'st the naked pathway to thy life,

Teaching sterne murther how to butcher thee:

That which in meane men we intitle patience

Is pale cold cowardice in noble brests:

What shall I say, to safegard thine owne life,

The best way is to venge my Glousters death

Gaunt. Heauens is the quarrell: for heauens substitute

His Deputy annointed in his sight,

Hath caus'd his death, the which if wrongfully

Let heauen reuenge: for I may neuer lift

An angry arme against his Minister

Dut. Where then (alas may I) complaint my selfe?

Gau. To heauen, the widdowes Champion to defence

Dut. Why then I will: farewell old Gaunt.

Thou go'st to Couentrie, there to behold

Our Cosine Herford, and fell Mowbray fight:

O sit my husbands wrongs on Herfords speare,

That it may enter butcher Mowbrayes brest:

Or if misfortune misse the first carreere,

Be Mowbrayes sinnes so heauy in his bosome,

That they may breake his foaming Coursers backe,

And throw the Rider headlong in the Lists,

A Caytiffe recreant to my Cosine Herford:

Farewell old Gaunt, thy sometimes brothers wife

With her companion Greefe, must end her life

Gau. Sister farewell: I must to Couentree,

As much good stay with thee, as go with mee

Dut. Yet one word more: Greefe boundeth where it falls,

Not with the emptie hollownes, but weight:

I take my leaue, before I haue begun,

For sorrow ends not, when it seemeth done.

Commend me to my brother Edmund Yorke.

Loe, this is all: nay, yet depart not so,

Though this be all, do not so quickly go,

I shall remember more. Bid him, Oh, what?

With all good speed at Plashie visit mee.

Alacke, and what shall good old Yorke there see

But empty lodgings, and vnfurnish'd walles,

Vn-peopel'd Offices, vntroden stones?

And what heare there for welcome, but my grones?

Therefore commend me, let him not come there,

To seeke out sorrow, that dwels euery where:

Desolate, desolate will I hence, and dye,

The last leaue of thee, takes my weeping eye.

> *Exeunt.*

Scena Tertia.

> *Enter Marshall, and Aumerle.*

Mar. My L[ord]. Aumerle, is Harry Herford arm'd

Aum. Yea, at all points, and longs to enter in

Mar. The Duke of Norfolke, sprightfully and bold,

Stayes but the summons of the Appealants Trumpet

Au. Why then the Champions, are prepar'd, and stay

For nothing but his Maiesties approach.

Flourish.

> *Enter King, Gaunt, Bushy, Bagot, Greene, & others: Then Mowbray in Armor, and Harrold.*

Rich. Marshall, demand of yonder Champion

The cause of his arriuall heere in Armes,

Aske him his name, and orderly proceed

To sweare him in the iustice of his cause

Mar. In Gods name, and the Kings say who y art,

And why thou com'st thus knightly clad in Armes?

Against what man thou com'st, and what's thy quarrell,

Speake truly on thy knighthood, and thine oath,

As so defend thee heauen, and thy valour

Mow. My name is Tho[mas]. Mowbray, Duke of Norfolk,

Who hither comes engaged by my oath

(Which heauen defend a knight should violate)

Both to defend my loyalty and truth,

To God, my King, and his succeeding issue,

Against the Duke of Herford, that appeales me:

And by the grace of God, and this mine arme,

To proue him (in defending of my selfe)

A Traitor to my God, my King, and me,

And as I truly fight, defend me heauen.

Tucket.

Enter Hereford, and Harold.

Rich. Marshall: Aske yonder Knight in Armes,

Both who he is, and why he commeth hither,

Thus placed in habiliments of warre:

And formerly according to our Law

Depose him in the iustice of his cause

Mar. What is thy name? and wherfore comst y hither

Before King Richard in his Royall Lists?

Against whom com'st thou? and what's thy quarrell?

Speake like a true Knight, so defend thee heauen

Bul. Harry of Herford, Lancaster, and Derbie,

Am I: who ready heere do stand in Armes,

To proue by heauens grace, and my bodies valour,

In Lists, on Thomas Mowbray Duke of Norfolke,

That he's a Traitor foule, and dangerous,

To God of heauen, King Richard, and to me,

And as I truly fight, defend me heauen

Mar. On paine of death, no person be so bold,

Or daring hardie as to touch the Listes,

Except the Marshall, and such Officers

Appointed to direct these faire designes

Bul. Lord Marshall, let me kisse my Soueraigns hand,

And bow my knee before his Maiestie:

For Mowbray and my selfe are like two men,

That vow a long and weary pilgrimage,

Then let vs take a ceremonious leaue

And louing farwell of our seuerall friends

Mar. The Appealant in all duty greets your Highnes,

And craues to kisse your hand, and take his leaue

Rich. We will descend, and fold him in our armes.

Cosin of Herford, as thy cause is iust,

So be thy fortune in this Royall fight:

Farewell, my blood, which if to day thou shead,

Lament we may, but not reuenge thee dead

Bull. Oh let no noble eye prophane a teare

For me, if I be gor'd with Mowbrayes speare:

As confident, as is the Falcons flight

Against a bird, do I with Mowbray fight.

My louing Lord, I take my leaue of you,

Of you (my Noble Cosin) Lord Aumerle;

Not sicke, although I haue to do with death,

But lustie, yong, and cheerely drawing breath.

Loe, as at English Feasts, so I regreete

The daintiest last, to make the end most sweet.

Oh thou the earthy author of my blood,

Whose youthfull spirit in me regenerate,

Doth with a two-fold rigor lift mee vp

To reach at victory aboue my head,

Adde proofe vnto mine Armour with thy prayres,

And with thy blessings steele my Lances point,

That it may enter Mowbrayes waxen Coate,

And furnish new the name of Iohn a Gaunt,

Euen in the lusty hauiour of his sonne

Gaunt. Heauen in thy good cause make thee prosp'rous

Be swift like lightning in the execution,

And let thy blowes doubly redoubled,

Fall like amazing thunder on the Caske

Of thy amaz'd pernicious enemy.

Rouze vp thy youthfull blood, be valiant, and liue

Bul. Mine innocence, and S[aint]. George to thriue

Mow. How euer heauen or fortune cast my lot,

There liues, or dies, true to Kings Richards Throne,

A loyall, iust, and vpright Gentleman:

Neuer did Captiue with a freer heart,

Cast off his chaines of bondage, and embrace

His golden vncontroul'd enfranchisement,

More then my dancing soule doth celebrate

This Feast of Battell, with mine Aduersarie.

Most mighty Liege, and my companion Peeres,

Take from my mouth, the wish of happy yeares,

As gentle, and as iocond, as to iest,

Go I to fight: Truth, hath a quiet brest

Rich. Farewell, my Lord, securely I espy

Vertue with Valour, couched in thine eye:

Order the triall Marshall, and begin

Mar. Harrie of Herford, Lancaster, and Derby,

Receiue thy Launce, and heauen defend thy right

Bul. Strong as a towre in hope, I cry Amen

Mar. Go beare this Lance to Thomas D[uke]. of Norfolke

1.Har. Harry of Herford, Lancaster, and Derbie,

Stands heere for God, his Soueraigne, and himselfe,

On paine to be found false, and recreant,

To proue the Duke of Norfolke, Thomas Mowbray,

A Traitor to his God, his King, and him,

And dares him to set forwards to the fight

2.Har. Here standeth Tho[mas]: Mowbray Duke of Norfolk

On paine to be found false and recreant,

Both to defend himselfe, and to approue

Henry of Herford, Lancaster, and Derby,

To God, his Soueraigne, and to him disloyall:

Couragiously, and with a free desire

Attending but the signall to begin.

A charge sounded

Mar. Sound Trumpets, and set forward Combatants:

Stay, the King hath throwne his Warder downe

Rich. Let them lay by their Helmets & their Speares,

And both returne backe to their Chaires againe:

Withdraw with vs, and let the Trumpets sound,

While we returne these Dukes what we decree.

A long Flourish.

Draw neere and list

What with our Councell we haue done.

For that our kingdomes earth should not be soyld

With that deere blood which it hath fostered,

And for our eyes do hate the dire aspect

Of ciuill wounds plowgh'd vp with neighbors swords,

Which so rouz'd vp with boystrous vntun'd drummes,

With harsh resounding Trumpets dreadfull bray,

And grating shocke of wrathfull yron Armes,

Might from our quiet Confines fright faire peace,

And make vs wade euen in our kindreds blood:

Therefore, we banish you our Territories.

You Cosin Herford, vpon paine of death,

Till twice fiue Summers haue enrich'd our fields,

Shall not regreet our faire dominions,

But treade the stranger pathes of banishment

Bul. Your will be done: This must my comfort be,

That Sun that warmes you heere, shall shine on me:

And those his golden beames to you heere lent,

Shall point on me, and gild my banishment

Rich. Norfolke: for thee remaines a heauier dombe,

Which I with some vnwillingnesse pronounce,

The slye slow houres shall not determinate

The datelesse limit of thy deere exile:

The hopelesse word, of Neuer to returne,

Breath I against thee, vpon paine of life

Mow. A heauy sentence, my most Soueraigne Liege,

And all vnlook'd for from your Highnesse mouth:

A deerer merit, not so deepe a maime,

As to be cast forth in the common ayre

Haue I deserued at your Highnesse hands.

The Language I haue learn'd these forty yeares

(My natiue English) now I must forgo,

And now my tongues vse is to me no more,

Then an vnstringed Vyall, or a Harpe,

Or like a cunning Instrument cas'd vp,

Or being open, put into his hands

That knowes no touch to tune the harmony.

Within my mouth you haue engaol'd my tongue,

Doubly percullist with my teeth and lippes,

And dull, vnfeeling, barren ignorance,

Is made my Gaoler to attend on me:

I am too old to fawne vpon a Nurse,

Too farre in yeeres to be a pupill now:

What is thy sentence then, but speechlesse death,

Which robs my tongue from breathing natiue breath?
Rich. It boots thee not to be compassionate,
After our sentence, plaining comes too late
Mow. Then thus I turne me from my countries light
To dwell in solemne shades of endlesse night
Ric. Returne againe, and take an oath with thee,
Lay on our Royall sword, your banisht hands;
Sweare by the duty that you owe to heauen
(Our part therein we banish with your selues)
To keepe the Oath that we administer:
You neuer shall (so helpe you Truth, and Heauen)
Embrace each others loue in banishment,
Nor euer looke vpon each others face,
Nor euer write, regreete, or reconcile
This lowring tempest of your home-bred hate,
Nor euer by aduised purpose meete,
To plot, contriue, or complot any ill,
'Gainst Vs, our State, our Subiects, or our Land
Bull. I sweare
Mow. And I, to keepe all this
Bul. Norfolke, so fare, as to mine enemie,
By this time (had the King permitted vs)
One of our soules had wandred in the ayre,
Banish'd this fraile sepulchre of our flesh,
As now our flesh is banish'd from this Land.
Confesse thy Treasons, ere thou flye this Realme,
Since thou hast farre to go, beare not along

The clogging burthen of a guilty soule

Mow. No Bullingbroke: If euer I were Traitor,

My name be blotted from the booke of Life,

And I from heauen banish'd, as from hence:

But what thou art, heauen, thou, and I do know,

And all too soone (I feare) the King shall rue.

Farewell (my Liege) now no way can I stray,

Saue backe to England, all the worlds my way.

   Enter.

Rich. Vncle, euen in the glasses of thine eyes

I see thy greeued heart: thy sad aspect,

Hath from the number of his banish'd yeares

Pluck'd foure away: Six frozen Winters spent,

Returne with welcome home, from banishment

Bul. How long a time lyes in one little word:

Foure lagging Winters, and foure wanton springs

End in a word, such is the breath of Kings

Gaunt. I thanke my Liege, that in regard of me

He shortens foure yeares of my sonnes exile:

But little vantage shall I reape thereby.

For ere the sixe yeares that he hath to spend

Can change their Moones, and bring their times about,

My oyle-dride Lampe, and time-bewasted light

Shall be extinct with age, and endlesse night:

My inch of Taper, will be burnt, and done,

And blindfold death, not let me see my sonne

Rich. Why Vncle, thou hast many yeeres to liue

Gaunt. But not a minute (King) that thou canst giue;

Shorten my dayes thou canst with sudden sorow,

And plucke nights from me, but not lend a morrow:

Thou canst helpe time to furrow me with age,

But stop no wrinkle in his pilgrimage:

Thy word is currant with him, for my death,

But dead, thy kingdome cannot buy my breath

Ric. Thy sonne is banish'd vpon good aduice,

Whereto thy tongue a party-verdict gaue,

Why at our Iustice seem'st thou then to lowre?

Gau. Things sweet to tast, proue in digestion sowre:

You vrg'd me as a Iudge, but I had rather

You would haue bid me argue like a Father.

Alas, I look'd when some of you should say,

I was too strict to make mine owne away:

But you gaue leaue to my vnwilling tong,

Against my will, to do my selfe this wrong

Rich. Cosine farewell: and Vncle bid him so:

Six yeares we banish him, and he shall go.

  Enter.

Flourish.

Au. Cosine farewell: what presence must not know

From where you do remaine, let paper show

Mar. My Lord, no leaue take I, for I will ride

As farre as land will let me, by your side

Gaunt. Oh to what purpose dost thou hord thy words,

That thou returnst no greeting to thy friends?

Bull. I haue too few to take my leaue of you,

When the tongues office should be prodigall,

To breath th' abundant dolour of the heart

Gau. Thy greefe is but thy absence for a time

Bull. Ioy absent, greefe is present for that time

Gau. What is sixe Winters, they are quickely gone?

Bul. To men in ioy, but greefe makes one houre ten

Gau. Call it a trauell that thou tak'st for pleasure

Bul. My heart will sigh, when I miscall it so,

Which findes it an inforced Pilgrimage

Gau. The sullen passage of thy weary steppes

Esteeme a soyle, wherein thou art to set

The precious Iewell of thy home returne

Bul. Oh who can hold a fire in his hand

By thinking on the frostie Caucasus?

Or cloy the hungry edge of appetite,

By bare imagination of a Feast?

Or Wallow naked in December snow

By thinking on fantasticke summers heate?

Oh no, the apprehension of the good

Giues but the greater feeling to the worse:

Fell sorrowes tooth, doth euer ranckle more

Then when it bites, but lanceth not the sore

Gau. Come, come (my son) Ile bring thee on thy way

Had I thy youth, and cause, I would not stay

Bul. Then Englands ground farewell: sweet soil adieu,

My Mother, and my Nurse, which beares me yet:

Where ere I wander, boast of this I can,
Though banish'd, yet a true-borne Englishman.

Scena Quarta.

Enter King, Aumerle, Greene, and Bagot.
Rich. We did obserue. Cosine Aumerle,
How far brought you high Herford on his way?
Aum. I brought high Herford (if you call him so)
But to the next high way, and there I left him
Rich. And say, what store of parting tears were shed?
Aum. Faith none for me: except the Northeast wind
Which then grew bitterly against our face,
Awak'd the sleepie rhewme, and so by chance
Did grace our hollow parting with a teare
Rich. What said our Cosin when you parted with him?
Au. Farewell: and for my hart disdained y my tongue
Should so prophane the word, that taught me craft
To counterfeit oppression of such greefe,
That word seem'd buried in my sorrowes graue.
Marry, would the word Farwell, haue lengthen'd houres,
And added yeeres to his short banishment,
He should haue had a volume of Farwels,
But since it would not, he had none of me
Rich. He is our Cosin (Cosin) but 'tis doubt,
When time shall call him home from banishment,
Whether our kinsman come to see his friends,
Our selfe, and Bushy: heere Bagot and Greene

Obseru'd his Courtship to the common people:

How he did seeme to diue into their hearts,

With humble, and familiar courtesie,

What reuerence he did throw away on slaues;

Wooing poore Craftes-men, with the craft of soules,

And patient vnder-bearing of his Fortune,

As 'twere to banish their affects with him.

Off goes his bonnet to an Oyster-wench,

A brace of Dray-men bid God speed him well,

And had the tribute of his supple knee,

With thankes my Countrimen, my louing friends,

As were our England in reuersion his,

And he our subiects next degree in hope

Gr. Well, he is gone, & with him go these thoughts:

Now for the Rebels, which stand out in Ireland,

Expedient manage must be made my Liege

Ere further leysure, yeeld them further meanes

For their aduantage, and your Highnesse losse

Ric. We will our selfe in person to this warre,

And for our Coffers, with too great a Court,

And liberall Largesse, are growne somewhat light,

We are inforc'd to farme our royall Realme,

The Reuennew whereof shall furnish vs

For our affayres in hand: if that come short

Our Substitutes at home shall haue Blanke-charters:

Whereto, when they shall know what men are rich,

They shall subscribe them for large summes of Gold,

And send them after to supply our wants:

For we will make for Ireland presently.

Enter Bushy.

Bushy, what newes?

Bu. Old Iohn of Gaunt is verie sicke my Lord,

Sodainly taken, and hath sent post haste

To entreat your Maiesty to visit him

Ric. Where lyes he?

Bu. At Ely house

Ric. Now put it (heauen) in his Physitians minde,

To helpe him to his graue immediately:

The lining of his coffers shall make Coates

To decke our souldiers for these Irish warres.

Come Gentlemen, let's all go visit him:

Pray heauen we may make hast, and come too late.

Enter.

Actus Secundus.

Scena Prima.

Enter Gaunt, sicke with Yorke.

Gau. Will the King come, that I may breath my last

In wholsome counsell to his vnstaid youth?

Yor. Vex not your selfe, nor striue not with your breth,

For all in vaine comes counsell to his eare

Gau. Oh but (they say) the tongues of dying men

Inforce attention like deepe harmony;

Where words are scarse, they are seldome spent in vaine,

For they breath truth, that breath their words in paine.

He that no more must say, is listen'd more,

Then they whom youth and ease haue taught to glose,

More are mens ends markt, then their liues before,

The setting Sun, and Musicke in the close

As the last taste of sweetes, is sweetest last,

Writ in remembrance, more then things long past;

Though Richard my liues counsell would not heare,

My deaths sad tale, may yet vndeafe his eare

Yor. No, it is stopt with other flatt'ring sounds

As praises of his state: then there are found

Lasciuious Meeters, to whose venom sound

The open eare of youth doth alwayes listen.

Report of fashions in proud Italy,

Whose manners still our tardie apish Nation

Limpes after in base imitation.

Where doth the world thrust forth a vanity,

So it be new, there's no respect how vile,

That is not quickly buz'd into his eares?

That all too late comes counsell to be heard,

Where will doth mutiny with wits regard:

Direct not him, whose way himselfe will choose,

Tis breath thou lackst, and that breath wilt thou loose

Gaunt. Me thinkes I am a Prophet new inspir'd,

And thus expiring, do foretell of him,

His rash fierce blaze of Ryot cannot last,

For violent fires soone burne out themselues,

Small showres last long, but sodaine stormes are short,

He tyres betimes, that spurs too fast betimes;

With eager feeding, food doth choake the feeder:

Light vanity, insatiate cormorant,

Consuming meanes soone preyes vpon it selfe.

This royall Throne of Kings, this sceptred Isle,

This earth of Maiesty, this seate of Mars,

This other Eden, demy paradise,

This Fortresse built by Nature for her selfe,

Against infection, and the hand of warre:

This happy breed of men, this little world,

This precious stone, set in the siluer sea,

Which serues it in the office of a wall,

Or as a Moate defensiue to a house,

Against the enuy of lesse happier Lands,

This blessed plot, this earth, this Realme, this England,

This Nurse, this teeming wombe of Royall Kings,

Fear'd by their breed, and famous for their birth,

Renowned for their deeds, as farre from home,

For Christian seruice, and true Chiualrie,

As is the sepulcher in stubborne Iury

Of the Worlds ransome, blessed Maries Sonne.

This Land of such deere soules, this deere-deere Land,

Deere for her reputation through the world,

Is now Leas'd out (I dye pronouncing it)

Like to a Tenement or pelting Farme.

England bound in with the triumphant sea,

Whose rocky shore beates backe the enuious siedge

Of watery Neptune, is now bound in with shame,

With Inky blottes, and rotten Parchment bonds.

That England, that was wont to conquer others,

Hath made a shamefull conquest of it selfe.

Ah! would the scandall vanish with my life,

How happy then were my ensuing death?

Enter King, Queene, Aumerle, Bushy, Greene, Bagot, Ros, and Willoughby.

Yor. The King is come, deale mildly with his youth,

For young hot Colts, being rag'd, do rage the more

Qu. How fares our noble Vncle Lancaster?

Ri. What comfort man? How ist with aged Gaunt?

Ga. Oh how that name befits my composition:

Old Gaunt indeed, and gaunt in being old:

Within me greefe hath kept a tedious fast,

And who abstaynes from meate, that is not gaunt?

For sleeping England long time haue I watcht,

Watching breeds leannesse, leannesse is all gaunt.

The pleasure that some Fathers feede vpon,

Is my strict fast, I meane my Childrens lookes,

And therein fasting, hast thou made me gaunt:

Gaunt am I for the graue, gaunt as a graue,

Whose hollow wombe inherits naught but bones

Ric. Can sicke men play so nicely with their names?

Gau. No, misery makes sport to mocke it selfe:

Since thou dost seeke to kill my name in mee,

I mocke my name (great King) to flatter thee
Ric. Should dying men flatter those that liue?
Gau. No, no, men liuing flatter those that dye
Rich. Thou now a dying, sayst thou flatter'st me
Gau. Oh no, thou dyest, though I the sicker be
Rich. I am in health, I breath, I see thee ill
Gau. Now he that made me, knowes I see thee ill:
Ill in my selfe to see, and in thee, seeing ill,
Thy death-bed is no lesser then the Land,
Wherein thou lyest in reputation sicke,
And thou too care-lesse patient as thou art,
Commit'st thy 'anointed body to the cure
Of those Physitians, that first wounded thee.
A thousand flatterers sit within thy Crowne,
Whose compasse is no bigger then thy head,
And yet incaged in so small a Verge,
The waste is no whit lesser then thy Land:
Oh had thy Grandsire with a Prophets eye,
Seene how his sonnes sonne, should destroy his sonnes,
From forth thy reach he would haue laid thy shame,
Deposing thee before thou wert possest,
Which art possest now to depose thy selfe.
Why (Cosine) were thou Regent of the world,
It were a shame to let his Land by lease:
But for thy world enioying but this Land,
Is it not more then shame, to shame it so?
Landlord of England art thou, and not King:

Thy state of Law, is bondslaue to the law,

And-

Rich. And thou, a lunaticke leane-witted foole,

Presuming on an Agues priuiledge,

Dar'st with thy frozen admonition

Make pale our cheeke, chasing the Royall blood

With fury, from his natiue residence?

Now by my Seates right Royall Maiestie,

Wer't thou not Brother to great Edwards sonne,

This tongue that runs so roundly in thy head,

Should run thy head from thy vnreuerent shoulders

Gau. Oh spare me not, my brothers Edwards sonne,

For that I was his Father Edwards sonne:

That blood already (like the Pellican)

Thou hast tapt out, and drunkenly carows'd.

My brother Gloucester, plaine well meaning soule

(Whom faire befall in heauen 'mongst happy soules)

May be a president, and witnesse good,

That thou respect'st not spilling Edwards blood:

Ioyne with the present sicknesse that I haue,

And thy vnkindnesse be like crooked age,

To crop at once a too-long wither'd flowre.

Liue in thy shame, but dye not shame with thee,

These words heereafter, thy tormentors bee.

Conuey me to my bed, then to my graue,

Loue they to liue, that loue and honor haue.

Exit

Rich. And let them dye, that age and sullens haue,

For both hast thou, and both become the graue

Yor. I do beseech your Maiestie impute his words

To wayward sicklinesse, and age in him:

He loues you on my life, and holds you deere

As Harry Duke of Herford, were he heere

Rich. Right, you say true: as Herfords loue, so his;

As theirs, so mine: and all be as it is.

Enter Northumberland.

Nor. My Liege, olde Gaunt commends him to your Maiestie

Rich. What sayes he?

Nor. Nay nothing, all is said:

His tongue is now a stringlesse instrument,

Words, life, and all, old Lancaster hath spent

Yor. Be Yorke the next, that must be bankrupt so,

Though death be poore, it ends a mortall wo

Rich. The ripest fruit first fals, and so doth he,

His time is spent, our pilgrimage must be:

So much for that. Now for our Irish warres,

We must supplant those rough rug-headed Kernes,

Which liue like venom, where no venom else

But onely they, haue priuiledge to liue.

And for these great affayres do aske some charge

Towards our assistance, we do seize to vs

The plate, coine, reuennewes, and moueables,

Whereof our Vncle Gaunt did stand possest

Yor. How long shall I be patient? Oh how long

Shall tender dutie make me suffer wrong?

Not Glousters death, nor Herfords banishment,

Nor Gauntes rebukes, nor Englands priuate wrongs,

Nor the preuention of poore Bullingbrooke,

About his marriage, nor my owne disgrace

Haue euer made me sowre my patient cheeke,

Or bend one wrinckle on my Soueraignes face:

I am the last of noble Edwards sonnes,

Of whom thy Father Prince of Wales was first,

In warre was neuer Lyon rag'd more fierce:

In peace, was neuer gentle Lambe more milde,

Then was that yong and Princely Gentleman,

His face thou hast, for euen so look'd he

Accomplish'd with the number of thy howers:

But when he frown'd, it was against the French,

And not against his friends: his noble hand

Did win what he did spend: and spent not that

Which his triumphant fathers hand had won:

His hands were guilty of no kindreds blood,

But bloody with the enemies of his kinne:

Oh Richard, Yorke is too farre gone with greefe,

Or else he neuer would compare betweene

Rich. Why Vncle,

What's the matter?

Yor. Oh my Liege, pardon me if you please, if not

I pleas'd not to be pardon'd, am content with all:

Seeke you to seize, and gripe into your hands
The Royalties and Rights of banish'd Herford?
Is not Gaunt dead? and doth not Herford liue?
Was not Gaunt iust? and is not Harry true?
Did not the one deserue to haue an heyre?
Is not his heyre a well-deseruing sonne?
Take Herfords rights away, and take from time
His Charters, and his customarie rights:
Let not to morrow then insue to day,
Be not thy selfe. For how art thou a King
But by faire sequence and succession?
Now afore God, God forbid I say true,
If you do wrongfully seize Herfords right,
Call in his Letters Patents that he hath
By his Atturneyes generall, to sue
His Liuerie, and denie his offer'd homage,
You plucke a thousand dangers on your head,
You loose a thousand well-disposed hearts,
And pricke my tender patience to those thoughts
Which honor and allegeance cannot thinke

Ric. Thinke what you will: we seise into our hands,
His plate, his goods, his money, and his lands

Yor. Ile not be by the while: My Liege farewell,
What will ensue heereof, there's none can tell.
But by bad courses may be vnderstood,
That their euents can neuer fall out good.
Enter.

Rich. Go Bushie to the Earle of Wiltshire streight,

Bid him repaire to vs to Ely house,

To see this businesse: to morrow next

We will for Ireland, and 'tis time, I trow:

And we create in absence of our selfe

Our Vncle Yorke, Lord Gouernor of England:

For he is iust, and alwayes lou'd vs well.

Come on our Queene, to morrow must we part,

Be merry, for our time of stay is short.

Flourish.

Manet North. Willoughby, & Ross.

Nor. Well Lords, the Duke of Lancaster is dead

Ross. And liuing too, for now his sonne is Duke

Wil. Barely in title, not in reuennew

Nor. Richly in both, if iustice had her right

Ross. My heart is great: but it must break with silence,

Er't be disburthen'd with a liberall tongue

Nor. Nay speake thy mind: & let him ne'r speak more

That speakes thy words againe to do thee harme

Wil. Tends that thou'dst speake to th' Du[ke]. of Hereford,

If it be so, out with it boldly man,

Quicke is mine eare to heare of good towards him

Ross. No good at all that I can do for him,

Vnlesse you call it good to pitie him,

Bereft and gelded of his patrimonie

Nor. Now afore heauen, 'tis shame such wrongs are borne.

In him a royall Prince, and many moe

Of noble blood in this declining Land;

The King is not himselfe, but basely led

By Flatterers, and what they will informe

Meerely in hate 'gainst any of vs all,

That will the King seuerely prosecute

'Gainst vs, our liues, our children, and our heires

Ros. The Commons hath he pil'd with greeuous taxes

And quite lost their hearts: the Nobles hath he finde

For ancient quarrels, and quite lost their hearts

Wil. And daily new exactions are deuis'd,

As blankes, beneuolences, and I wot not what:

But what o' Gods name doth become of this?

Nor. Wars hath not wasted it, for war'd he hath not.

But basely yeelded vpon comprimize,

That which his Ancestors atchieu'd with blowes:

More hath he spent in peace, then they in warres

Ros. The Earle of Wiltshire hath the realme in Farme

Wil. The Kings growne bankrupt like a broken man

Nor. Reproach, and dissolution hangeth ouer him

Ros. He hath not monie for these Irish warres:

(His burthenous taxations notwithstanding)

But by the robbing of the banish'd Duke

Nor. His noble Kinsman, most degenerate King:

But Lords, we heare this fearefull tempest sing,

Yet seeke no shelter to auoid the storme:

We see the winde sit sore vpon our sailes,

And yet we strike not, but securely perish

Ros. We see the very wracke that we must suffer,

And vnauoyded is the danger now

For suffering so the causes of our wracke

Nor. Not so: euen through the hollow eyes of death,

I spie life peering: but I dare not say

How neere the tidings of our comfort is

Wil. Nay let vs share thy thoughts, as thou dost ours

Ros. Be confident to speake Northumberland,

We three, are but thy selfe, and speaking so,

Thy words are but as thoughts, therefore be bold

Nor. Then thus: I haue from Port le Blan

A Bay in Britaine, receiu'd intelligence,

That Harry Duke of Herford, Rainald Lord Cobham,

That late broke from the Duke of Exeter,

His brother Archbishop, late of Canterbury,

Sir Thomas Erpingham, Sir Iohn Rainston,

Sir Iohn Norberie, & Sir Robert Waterton, & Francis Quoint,

All these well furnish'd by the Duke of Britaine,

With eight tall ships, three thousand men of warre

Are making hither with all due expedience,

And shortly meane to touch our Northerne shore:

Perhaps they had ere this, but that they stay

The first departing of the King for Ireland.

If then we shall shake off our slauish yoake,

Impe out our drooping Countries broken wing,

Redeeme from broaking pawne the blemish'd Crowne,

Wipe off the dust that hides our Scepters gilt,
And make high Maiestie looke like it selfe,
Away with me in poste to Rauenspurgh,
But if you faint, as fearing to do so,
Stay, and be secret, and my selfe will go
Ros. To horse, to horse, vrge doubts to them y feare
Wil. Hold out my horse, and I will first be there.
   Exeunt.

Scena Secunda.

Enter Queene, Bushy, and Bagot.
Bush. Madam, your Maiesty is too much sad,
You promis'd when you parted with the King,
To lay aside selfe-harming heauinesse,
And entertaine a cheerefull disposition
Qu. To please the King, I did: to please my selfe
I cannot do it: yet I know no cause
Why I should welcome such a guest as greefe,
Saue bidding farewell to so sweet a guest
As my sweet Richard; yet againe me thinkes,
Some vnborne sorrow, ripe in fortunes wombe
Is comming towards me, and my inward soule
With nothing trembles, at something it greeues,
More then with parting from my Lord the King
Bush. Each substance of a greefe hath twenty shadows
Which shewes like greefe it selfe, but is not so:
For sorrowes eye, glazed with blinding teares,

Diuides one thing intire, to many obiects,

Like perspectiues, which rightly gaz'd vpon

Shew nothing but confusion, ey'd awry,

Distinguish forme: so your sweet Maiestie

Looking awry vpon your Lords departure,

Finde shapes of greefe, more then himselfe to waile,

Which look'd on as it is, is naught but shadowes

Of what it is not: then thrice-gracious Queene,

More then your Lords departure weep not, more's not seene;

Or if it be, 'tis with false sorrowes eie,

Which for things true, weepe things imaginary

Qu. It may be so: but yet my inward soule

Perswades me it is otherwise: how ere it be,

I cannot but be sad: so heauy sad,

As though on thinking on no thought I thinke,

Makes me with heauy nothing faint and shrinke

Bush. 'Tis nothing but conceit (my gracious Lady.)

Qu. 'Tis nothing lesse: conceit is still deriu'd

From some fore-father greefe, mine is not so,

For nothing hath begot my something greefe,

Or something, hath the nothing that I greeue,

'Tis in reuersion that I do possesse,

But what it is, that is not yet knowne, what

I cannot name, 'tis namelesse woe I wot.

Enter Greene.

Gree. Heauen saue your Maiesty, and wel met Gentlemen:

I hope the King is not yet shipt for Ireland

Qu. Why hop'st thou so? Tis better hope he is:

For his designes craue hast, his hast good hope,

Then wherefore dost thou hope he is not shipt?

Gre. That he our hope, might haue retyr'd his power,

and driuen into dispaire an enemies hope,

Who strongly hath set footing in this Land.

The banish'd Bullingbrooke repeales himselfe,

And with vp-lifted Armes is safe arriu'd

At Rauenspurg

Qu. Now God in heauen forbid

Gr. O Madam 'tis too true: and that is worse,

The L[ord]. Northumberland, his yong sonne Henrie Percie,

The Lords of Rosse, Beaumond, and Willoughby,

With all their powrefull friends are fled to him

Bush. Why haue you not proclaim'd Northumberland

And the rest of the reuolted faction, Traitors?

Gre. We haue: whereupon the Earle of Worcester

Hath broke his staffe, resign'd his Stewardship,

And al the houshold seruants fled with him to Bullinbrook

Qu. So Greene, thou art the midwife of my woe,

And Bullinbrooke my sorrowes dismall heyre:

Now hath my soule brought forth her prodegie,

And I a gasping new deliuered mother,

Haue woe to woe, sorrow to sorrow ioyn'd

Bush. Dispaire not Madam

Qu. Who shall hinder me?

I will dispaire, and be at enmitie

With couzening hope; he is a Flatterer,

A Parasite, a keeper backe of death,

Who gently would dissolue the bands of life,

Which false hopes linger in extremity.

Enter Yorke.

Gre. Heere comes the Duke of Yorke

Qu. With signes of warre about his aged necke,

Oh full of carefull businesse are his lookes:

Vncle, for heauens sake speake comfortable words:

Yor. Comfort's in heauen, and we are on the earth,

Where nothing liues but crosses, care and greefe:

Your husband he is gone to saue farre off,

Whilst others come to make him loose at home:

Heere am I left to vnder-prop his Land,

Who weake with age, cannot support my selfe:

Now comes the sicke houre that his surfet made,

Now shall he try his friends that flattered him.

Enter a seruant.

Ser. My Lord, your sonne was gone before I came

Yor. He was: why so: go all which way it will:

The Nobles they are fled, the Commons they are cold,

And will I feare reuolt on Herfords side.

Sirra, get thee to Plashie to my sister Gloster,

Bid her send me presently a thousand pound,

Hold, take my Ring

Ser. My Lord, I had forgot

To tell your Lordship, to day I came by, and call'd there,

But I shall greeue you to report the rest

Yor. What is't knaue?

Ser. An houre before I came, the Dutchesse di'de

Yor. Heau'n for his mercy, what a tide of woes

Come rushing on this wofull Land at once?

I know not what to do: I would to heauen

(So my vntruth had not prouok'd him to it)

The King had cut off my head with my brothers.

What, are there postes dispatcht for Ireland?

How shall we do for money for these warres?

Come sister (Cozen I would say) pray pardon me.

Go fellow, get thee home, prouide some Carts,

And bring away the Armour that is there.

Gentlemen, will you muster men?

If I know how, or which way to order these affaires

Thus disorderly thrust into my hands,

Neuer beleeue me. Both are my kinsmen,

Th' one is my Soueraigne, whom both my oath

And dutie bids defend: th' other againe

Is my kinsman, whom the King hath wrong'd,

Whom conscience, and my kindred bids to right:

Well, somewhat we must do: Come Cozen,

Ile dispose of you. Gentlemen, go muster vp your men,

And meet me presently at Barkley Castle:

I should to Plashy too: but time will not permit,

All is vneuen, and euery thing is left at six and seuen.

Exit

Bush. The winde sits faire for newes to go to Ireland,

But none returnes: For vs to leuy power

Proportionable to th' enemy, is all impossible

Gr. Besides our neerenesse to the King in loue,

Is neere the hate of those loue not the King

Ba. And that's the wauering Commons, for their loue

Lies in their purses, and who so empties them,

By so much fils their hearts with deadly hate

Bush. Wherein the king stands generally condemn'd

Bag. If iudgement lye in them, then so do we,

Because we haue beene euer neere the King

Gr. Well: I will for refuge straight to Bristoll Castle,

The Earle of Wiltshire is alreadie there

Bush. Thither will I with you, for little office

Will the hatefull Commons performe for vs,

Except like Curres, to teare vs all in peeces:

Will you go along with vs?

Bag. No, I will to Ireland to his Maiestie:

Farewell, if hearts presages be not vaine,

We three here part, that neu'r shall meete againe

Bu. That's as Yorke thriues to beate back Bullinbroke

Gr. Alas poore Duke, the taske he vndertakes

Is numbring sands, and drinking Oceans drie,

Where one on his side fights, thousands will flye

Bush. Farewell at once, for once, for all, and euer.

Well, we may meete againe

Bag. I feare me neuer.

Enter.

Scena Tertia.

Enter the Duke of Hereford, and Northumberland.

Bul. How farre is it my Lord to Berkley now?

Nor. Beleeue me noble Lord,

I am a stranger heere in Gloustershire,

These high wilde hilles, and rough vneeuen waies,

Drawes out our miles, and makes them wearisome.

And yet our faire discourse hath beene as sugar,

Making the hard way sweet and delectable:

But I bethinke me, what a wearie way

From Rauenspurgh to Cottshold will be found,

In Rosse and Willoughby, wanting your companie,

Which I protest hath very much beguild

The tediousnesse, and processe of my trauell:

But theirs is sweetned with the hope to haue

The present benefit that I possesse;

And hope to ioy, is little lesse in ioy,

Then hope enioy'd: By this, the wearie Lords

Shall make their way seeme short, as mine hath done,

By sight of what I haue, your Noble Companie

Bull. Of much lesse value is my Companie,

Then your good words: but who comes here?

Enter H[arry]. Percie.

North. It is my Sonne, young Harry Percie,

Sent from my Brother Worcester: Whence soeuer.

Harry, how fares your Vnckle?

Percie. I had thought, my Lord, to haue learn'd his
health of you

North. Why, is he not with the Queene?

Percie. No, my good Lord, he hath forsook the Court,
Broken his Staffe of Office, and disperst
The Household of the King

North. What was his reason?
He was not so resolu'd, when we last spake together

Percie. Because your Lordship was proclaimed Traitor.
But hee, my Lord, is gone to Rauenspurgh,
To offer seruice to the Duke of Hereford,
And sent me ouer by Barkely, to discouer
What power the Duke of Yorke had leuied there,
Then with direction to repaire to Rauenspurgh

North. Haue you forgot the Duke of Hereford (Boy.)

Percie. No, my good Lord; for that is not forgot
Which ne're I did remember: to my knowledge,
I neuer in my life did looke on him

North. Then learne to know him now: this is the
Duke

Percie. My gracious Lord, I tender you my seruice,
Such as it is, being tender, raw, and young,
Which elder dayes shall ripen, and confirme
To more approued seruice, and desert

Bull. I thanke thee gentle Percie, and be sure
I count my selfe in nothing else so happy,

As in a Soule remembring my good Friends:
And as my Fortune ripens with thy Loue,
It shall be still thy true Loues recompence,
My Heart this Couenant makes, my Hand thus seales it
North. How farre is it to Barkely? and what stirre
Keepes good old Yorke there, with his Men of Warre?
Percie. There stands the Castle, by yond tuft of Trees,
Mann'd with three hundred men, as I haue heard,
And in it are the Lords of Yorke, Barkely, and Seymor,
None else of Name, and noble estimate.
Enter Rosse and Willoughby.
North. Here come the Lords of Rosse and Willoughby,
Bloody with spurring, fierie red with haste
Bull. Welcome my Lords, I wot your loue pursues
A banisht Traytor; all my Treasurie
Is yet but vnfelt thankes, which more enrich'd,
Shall be your loue, and labours recompence
Ross. Your presence makes vs rich, most Noble Lord
Willo. And farre surmounts our labour to attaine it
Bull. Euermore thankes, th' Exchequer of the poore,
Which till my infant-fortune comes to yeeres,
Stands for my Bountie: but who comes here?
Enter Barkely.
North. It is my Lord of Barkely, as I ghesse
Bark. My Lord of Hereford, my Message is to you
Bull. My Lord, my Answere is to Lancaster,
And I am come to seeke that Name in England,

And I must finde that Title in your Tongue,

Before I make reply to aught you say

Bark. Mistake me not, my Lord, 'tis not my meaning

To raze one Title of your Honor out.

To you, my Lord, I come (what Lord you will)

From the most glorious of this Land,

The Duke of Yorke, to know what pricks you on

To take aduantage of the absent time,

And fright our Natiue Peace with selfe-borne Armes.

Enter Yorke.

Bull. I shall not need transport my words by you,

Here comes his Grace in Person. My Noble Vnckle

York. Shew me thy humble heart, and not thy knee,

Whose dutie is deceiuable, and false

Bull. My gracious Vnckle

York. Tut, tut, Grace me no Grace, nor Vnckle me,

I am no Traytors Vnckle; and that word Grace,

In an vngracious mouth, is but prophane.

Why haue these banish'd, and forbidden Legges,

Dar'd once to touch a Dust of Englands Ground?

But more then why, why haue they dar'd to march

So many miles vpon her peacefull Bosome,

Frighting her pale-fac'd Villages with Warre,

And ostentation of despised Armes?

Com'st thou because th' anoynted King is hence?

Why foolish Boy, the King is left behind,

And in my loyall Bosome lyes his power.

Were I but now the Lord of such hot youth,
As when braue Gaunt, thy Father, and my selfe
Rescued the Black Prince, that yong Mars of men,
From forth the Rankes of many thousand French:
Oh then, how quickly should this Arme of mine,
Now Prisoner to the Palsie, chastise thee,
And minister correction to thy Fault

Bull. My gracious Vnckle, let me know my Fault,
On what Condition stands it, and wherein?

York. Euen in Condition of the worst degree,
In grosse Rebellion, and detested Treason:
Thou art a banish'd man, and here art come
Before th' expiration of thy time,
In brauing Armes against thy Soueraigne

Bull. As I was banish'd, I was banish'd Hereford,
But as I come, I come for Lancaster.
And Noble Vnckle, I beseech your Grace
Looke on my Wrongs with an indifferent eye:
You are my Father, for me thinkes in you
I see old Gaunt aliue. Oh then my Father,
Will you permit, that I shall stand condemn'd
A wandring Vagabond; my Rights and Royalties
Pluckt from my armes perforce, and giuen away
To vpstart Vnthrifts? Wherefore was I borne?
If that my Cousin King, be King of England,
It must be graunted, I am Duke of Lancaster.
You haue a Sonne, Aumerle, my Noble Kinsman,

Had you first died, and he beene thus trod downe,
He should haue found his Vnckle Gaunt a Father,
To rowze his Wrongs, and chase them to the bay.
I am denyde to sue my Liuerie here,
And yet my Letters Patents giue me leaue:
My Fathers goods are all distraynd, and sold,
And these, and all, are all amisse imployd.
What would you haue me doe? I am a Subiect,
And challenge Law: Attorneyes are deny'd me;
And therefore personally I lay my claime
To my Inheritance of free Discent
North. The Noble Duke hath been too much abus'd
Ross. It stands your Grace vpon, to doe him right
Willo. Base men by his endowments are made great
York. My Lords of England, let me tell you this,
I haue had feeling of my Cosens Wrongs,
And labour'd all I could to doe him right:
But in this kind, to come in brauing Armes,
Be his owne Caruer, and cut out his way,
To find out Right with Wrongs, it may not be;
And you that doe abett him in this kind,
Cherish Rebellion, and are Rebels all
North. The Noble Duke hath sworne his comming is
But for his owne; and for the right of that,
Wee all haue strongly sworne to giue him ayd,
And let him neu'r see Ioy, that breakes that Oath
York. Well, well, I see the issue of these Armes,

I cannot mend it, I must needes confesse,
Because my power is weake, and all ill left:
But if I could, by him that gaue me life,
I would attach you all, and make you stoope
Vnto the Soueraigne Mercy of the King.
But since I cannot, be it knowne to you,
I doe remaine as Neuter. So fare you well,
Vnlesse you please to enter in the Castle,
And there repose you for this Night
  Bull. An offer Vnckle, that wee will accept:
But wee must winne your Grace to goe with vs
To Bristow Castle, which they say is held
By Bushie, Bagot, and their Complices,
The Caterpillers of the Commonwealth,
Which I haue sworne to weed, and plucke away
  York. It may be I will go with you: but yet Ile pawse,
For I am loth to breake our Countries Lawes:
Nor Friends, nor Foes, to me welcome you are,
Things past redresse, are now with me past care.
  Exeunt.

Scena Quarta.

Enter Salisbury, and a Captaine.

  Capt. My Lord of Salisbury, we haue stayd ten dayes,
And hardly kept our Countreymen together,
And yet we heare no tidings from the King;
Therefore we will disperse our selues: farewell

Sal. Stay yet another day, thou trustie Welchman,

The King reposeth all his confidence in thee

Capt. 'Tis thought the King is dead, we will not stay;

The Bay-trees in our Countrey all are wither'd,

And Meteors fright the fixed Starres of Heauen;

The pale-fac'd Moone lookes bloody on the Earth,

And leane-look'd Prophets whisper fearefull change;

Rich men looke sad, and Ruffians dance and leape,

The one in feare, to loose what they enioy,

The other to enioy by Rage, and Warre:

These signes fore-run the death of Kings.

Farewell, our Countreymen are gone and fled,

As well assur'd Richard their King is dead.

Enter.

Sal. Ah Richard, with eyes of heauie mind,

I see thy Glory, like a shooting Starre,

Fall to the base Earth, from the Firmament:

Thy Sunne sets weeping in the lowly West,

Witnessing Stormes to come, Woe, and Vnrest:

Thy Friends are fled, to wait vpon thy Foes,

And crossely to thy good, all fortune goes.

Enter.

Actus Tertius.

Scena Prima.

Enter Bullingbrooke, Yorke, Northumberland, Rosse, Percie, Willoughby, with Bushie and Greene Prisoners.

Bull. Bring forth these men:

Bushie and Greene, I will not vex your soules,

(Since presently your soules must part your bodies)

With too much vrging your pernitious liues,

For 'twere no Charitie: yet to wash your blood

From off my hands, here in the view of men,

I will vnfold some causes of your deaths.

You haue mis-led a Prince, a Royall King,

A happie Gentleman in Blood, and Lineaments,

By you vnhappied, and disfigur'd cleane:

You haue in manner with your sinfull houres

Made a Diuorce betwixt his Queene and him,

Broke the possession of a Royall Bed,

And stayn'd the beautie of a faire Queenes Cheekes,

With teares drawn fro[m] her eyes, with your foule wrongs.

My selfe a Prince, by fortune of my birth,

Neere to the King in blood, and neere in loue,

Till you did make him mis-interprete me,

Haue stoopt my neck vnder your iniuries,

And sigh'd my English breath in forraine Clouds,

Eating the bitter bread of banishment;

While you haue fed vpon my Seignories,

Dis-park'd my Parkes, and fell'd my Forrest Woods;

From mine owne Windowes torne my Household Coat,

Raz'd out my Impresse, leauing me no signe,

Saue mens opinions, and my liuing blood,

To shew the World I am a Gentleman.

This, and much more, much more then twice all this,
Condemnes you to the death: see them deliuered ouer
To execution, and the hand of death

Bushie. More welcome is the stroake of death to me,
Then Bullingbrooke to England

Greene. My comfort is, that Heauen will take our soules,
And plague Iniustice with the paines of Hell

Bull. My Lord Northumberland, see them dispatch'd:
Vnckle, you say the Queene is at your House,
For Heauens sake fairely let her be entreated,
Tell her I send to her my kind commends;
Take speciall care my Greetings be deliuer'd

York. A Gentleman of mine I haue dispatch'd
With Letters of your loue, to her at large

Bull. Thankes gentle Vnckle: come Lords away,
To fight with Glendoure, and his Complices;
A while to worke, and after holliday.

    Exeunt.

Scena Secunda.

Drums: Flourish, and Colours. Enter Richard, Aumerle, Carlile, and
Souldiers.

Rich. Barkloughly Castle call you this at hand?
Au. Yea, my Lord: how brooks your Grace the ayre,
After your late tossing on the breaking Seas?
Rich. Needs must I like it well: I weepe for ioy

To stand vpon my Kingdome once againe.

Deere Earth, I doe salute thee with my hand,

Though Rebels wound thee with their Horses hoofes:

As a long parted Mother with her Child,

Playes fondly with her teares, and smiles in meeting;

So weeping, smiling, greet I thee my Earth,

And doe thee fauor with my Royall hands.

Feed not thy Soueraignes Foe, my gentle Earth,

Nor with thy Sweetes, comfort his rauenous sence:

But let thy Spiders, that suck vp thy Venome,

And heauie-gated Toades lye in their way,

Doing annoyance to the trecherous feete,

Which with vsurping steps doe trample thee.

Yeeld stinging Nettles to mine Enemies;

And when they from thy Bosome pluck a Flower,

Guard it I prethee with a lurking Adder,

Whose double tongue may with a mortall touch

Throw death vpon thy Soueraignes Enemies.

Mock not my sencelesse Coniuration, Lords;

This Earth shall haue a feeling, and these Stones

Proue armed Souldiers, ere her Natiue King

Shall falter vnder foule Rebellious Armes

Car. Feare not my Lord, that Power that made you King

Hath power to keepe you King, in spight of all

Aum. He meanes, my Lord, that we are too remisse,

Whilest Bullingbrooke through our securitie,

Growes strong and great, in substance and in friends

Rich. Discomfortable Cousin, knowest thou not,

That when the searching Eye of Heauen is hid

Behind the Globe, that lights the lower World,

Then Theeues and Robbers raunge abroad vnseene,

In Murthers and in Out-rage bloody here:

But when from vnder this Terrestriall Ball

He fires the prowd tops of the Easterne Pines,

And darts his Lightning through eu'ry guiltie hole,

Then Murthers, Treasons, and detested sinnes

(The Cloake of Night being pluckt from off their backs)

Stand bare and naked, trembling at themselues.

So when this Theefe, this Traytor Bullingbrooke,

Who all this while hath reuell'd in the Night,

Shall see vs rising in our Throne, the East,

His Treasons will sit blushing in his face,

Not able to endure the sight of Day;

But selfe-affrighted, tremble at his sinne.

Not all the Water in the rough rude Sea

Can wash the Balme from an anoynted King;

The breath of worldly men cannot depose

The Deputie elected by the Lord:

For euery man that Bullingbrooke hath prest,

To lift shrewd Steele against our Golden Crowne,

Heauen for his Richard hath in heauenly pay

A glorious Angell: then if Angels fight,

Weake men must fall, for Heauen still guards the right.

Enter Salisbury.

Welcome my Lord, how farre off lyes your Power?

Salisb. Nor neere, nor farther off, my gracious Lord,

Then this weake arme; discomfort guides my tongue,

And bids me speake of nothing but despaire:

One day too late, I feare (my Noble Lord)

Hath clouded all thy happie dayes on Earth:

Oh call backe Yesterday, bid Time returne,

And thou shalt haue twelue thousand fighting men:

To day, to day, vnhappie day too late

Orethrowes thy Ioyes, Friends, Fortune, and thy State;

For all the Welchmen hearing thou wert dead,

Are gone to Bullingbrooke, disperst, and fled

Aum. Comfort my Liege, why lookes your Grace so pale?

Rich. But now the blood of twentie thousand men

Did triumph in my face, and they are fled,

And till so much blood thither come againe,

Haue I not reason to looke pale, and dead?

All Soules that will be safe, flye from my side,

For Time hath set a blot vpon my pride

Aum. Comfort my Liege, remember who you are

Rich. I had forgot my selfe. Am I not King?

Awake thou sluggard Maiestie, thou sleepest:

Is not the Kings Name fortie thousand Names?

Arme, arme my Name: a punie subiect strikes

At thy great glory. Looke not to the ground,

Ye Fauorites of a King: are wee not high?

High be our thoughts: I know my Vnckle Yorke

Hath Power enough to serue our turne.

But who comes here?

Enter Scroope.

Scroope. More health and happinesse betide my Liege,

Then can my care-tun'd tongue deliuer him

Rich. Mine eare is open, and my heart prepar'd:

The worst is worldly losse, thou canst vnfold:

Say, Is my Kingdome lost? why 'twas my Care:

And what losse is it to be rid of Care?

Striues Bullingbrooke to be as Great as wee?

Greater he shall not be: If hee serue God,

Wee'l serue him too, and be his Fellow so.

Reuolt our Subiects? That we cannot mend,

They breake their Faith to God, as well as vs:

Cry Woe, Destruction, Ruine, Losse, Decay,

The worst is Death, and Death will haue his day

Scroope. Glad am I, that your Highnesse is so arm'd

To beare the tidings of Calamitie.

Like an vnseasonable stormie day,

Which make the Siluer Riuers drowne their Shores,

As if the World were all dissolu'd to teares:

So high, aboue his Limits, swells the Rage

Of Bullingbrooke, couering your fearefull Land

With hard bright Steele, and hearts harder then Steele:

White Beares haue arm'd their thin and hairelesse Scalps

Against thy Maiestie, and Boyes with Womens Voyces,

Striue to speake bigge, and clap their female ioints
In stiffe vnwieldie Armes: against thy Crowne
Thy very Beads-men learne to bend their Bowes
Of double fatall Eugh: against thy State
Yea Distaffe-Women manage rustie Bills:
Against thy Seat both young and old rebell,
And all goes worse then I haue power to tell
Rich. Too well, too well thou tell'st a Tale so ill.
Where is the Earle of Wiltshire? where is Bagot?
What is become of Bushie? where is Greene?
That they haue let the dangerous Enemie
Measure our Confines with such peacefull steps?
If we preuaile, their heads shall pay for it.
I warrant they haue made peace with Bullingbrooke
Scroope. Peace haue they made with him indeede (my Lord.)
Rich. Oh Villains, Vipers, damn'd without redemption,
Dogges, easily woon to fawne on any man,
Snakes in my heart blood warm'd, that sting my heart,
Three Iudasses, each one thrice worse then Iudas,
Would they make peace? terrible Hell make warre
Vpon their spotted Soules for this Offence
Scroope. Sweet Loue (I see) changing his propertie,
Turnes to the sowrest, and most deadly hate:
Againe vncurse their Soules; their peace is made
With Heads, and not with Hands: those whom you curse
Haue felt the worst of Deaths destroying hand,

And lye full low, grau'd in the hollow ground
Aum. Is Bushie, Greene, and the Earle of Wiltshire dead?
Scroope. Yea, all of them at Bristow lost their heads
Aum. Where is the Duke my Father with his Power?
Rich. No matter where; of comfort no man speake:
Let's talke of Graues, of Wormes, and Epitaphs,
Make Dust our Paper, and with Raynie eyes
Write Sorrow on the Bosome of the Earth.
Let's chuse Executors, and talke of Wills:
And yet not so; for what can we bequeath,
Saue our deposed bodies to the ground?
Our Lands, our Liues, and all are Bullingbrookes,
And nothing can we call our owne, but Death,
And that small Modell of the barren Earth,
Which serues as Paste, and Couer to our Bones:
For Heauens sake let vs sit vpon the ground,
And tell sad stories of the death of Kings:
How some haue been depos'd, some slaine in warre,
Some haunted by the Ghosts they haue depos'd,
Some poyson'd by their Wiues, some sleeping kill'd,
All murther'd. For within the hollow Crowne
That rounds the mortall Temples of a King,
Keepes Death his Court, and there the Antique sits
Scoffing his State, and grinning at his Pompe,
Allowing him a breath, a little Scene,
To Monarchize, be fear'd, and kill with lookes,

Infusing him with selfe and vaine conceit,

As if this Flesh, which walls about our Life,

Were Brasse impregnable: and humor'd thus,

Comes at the last, and with a little Pinne

Bores through his Castle Walls, and farwell King.

Couer your heads, and mock not flesh and blood

With solemne Reuerence: throw away Respect,

Tradition, Forme, and Ceremonious dutie,

For you haue but mistooke me all this while:

I liue with Bread like you, feele Want,

Taste Griefe, need Friends: subiected thus,

How can you say to me, I am a King?

Carl. My Lord, wise men ne're waile their present woes,

But presently preuent the wayes to waile:

To feare the Foe, since feare oppresseth strength,

Giues in your weakenesse, strength vnto your Foe;

Feare, and be slaine, no worse can come to sight,

And fight and die, is death destroying death,

Where fearing, dying, payes death seruile breath

Aum. My Father hath a Power, enquire of him;

And learne to make a Body of a Limbe

Rich. Thou chid'st me well: proud Bullingbrooke I come

To change Blowes with thee, for our day of Doome:

This ague fit of feare is ouer-blowne,

An easie taske it is to winne our owne.

Say Scroope, where lyes our Vnckle with his Power?

Speake sweetly man, although thy lookes be sowre

Scroope. Men iudge by the complexion of the Skie

The state and inclination of the day;

So may you by my dull and heauie Eye:

My Tongue hath but a heauier Tale to say:

I play the Torturer, by small and small

To lengthen out the worst, that must be spoken.

Your Vnckle Yorke is ioyn'd with Bullingbrooke,

And all your Northerne Castles yeelded vp,

And all your Southerne Gentlemen in Armes

Vpon his Faction

Rich. Thou hast said enough.

Beshrew thee Cousin, which didst lead me forth

Of that sweet way I was in, to despaire:

What say you now? What comfort haue we now?

By Heauen Ile hate him euerlastingly,

That bids me be of comfort any more.

Goe to Flint Castle, there Ile pine away,

A King, Woes slaue, shall Kingly Woe obey:

That Power I haue, discharge, and let 'em goe

To eare the Land, that hath some hope to grow,

For I haue none. Let no man speake againe

To alter this, for counsaile is but vaine

Aum. My Liege, one word

Rich. He does me double wrong,

That wounds me with the flatteries of his tongue.

Discharge my followers: let them hence away,

From Richards Night, to Bullingbrookes faire Day.

Exeunt.

Scena Tertia.

Enter with Drum and Colours, Bullingbrooke, Yorke,
Northumberland,
Attendants.

Bull. So that by this intelligence we learne
The Welchmen are dispers'd, and Salisbury
Is gone to meet the King, who lately landed
With some few priuate friends, vpon this Coast
North. The newes is very faire and good, my Lord,
Richard, not farre from hence, hath hid his head
York. It would beseeme the Lord Northumberland,
To say King Richard: alack the heauie day,
When such a sacred King should hide his head
North. Your Grace mistakes: onely to be briefe,
Left I his Title out
York. The time hath beene,
Would you haue beene so briefe with him, he would
Haue beene so briefe with you, to shorten you,
For taking so the Head, your whole heads length
Bull. Mistake not (Vnckle) farther then you should
York. Take not (good Cousin) farther then you should.
Least you mistake the Heauens are ore your head
Bull. I know it (Vnckle) and oppose not my selfe
Against their will. But who comes here?
Enter Percie.

Welcome Harry: what, will not this Castle yeeld?

Per. The Castle royally is mann'd, my Lord,

Against thy entrance

Bull. Royally? Why, it containes no King?

Per. Yes (my good Lord)

It doth containe a King: King Richard lyes

Within the limits of yond Lime and Stone,

And with him, the Lord Aumerle, Lord Salisbury,

Sir Stephen Scroope, besides a Clergie man

Of holy reuerence; who, I cannot learne

North. Oh, belike it is the Bishop of Carlile

Bull. Noble Lord,

Goe to the rude Ribs of that ancient Castle,

Through Brazen Trumpet send the breath of Parle

Into his ruin'd Eares, and thus deliuer:

Henry Bullingbrooke vpon his knees doth kisse

King Richards hand, and sends allegeance

And true faith of heart to his Royall Person: hither come

Euen at his feet, to lay my Armes and Power,

Prouided, that my Banishment repeal'd,

And Lands restor'd againe, be freely graunted:

If not, Ile vse th 'aduantage of my Power,

And lay the Summers dust with showers of blood,

Rayn'd from the wounds of slaughter'd Englishmen;

The which, how farre off from the mind of Bullingbrooke

It is, such Crimson Tempest should bedrench

The fresh greene Lap of faire King Richards Land,

My stooping dutie tenderly shall shew.

Goe signifie as much, while here we march

Vpon the Grassie Carpet of this Plaine:

Let's march without the noyse of threatning Drum,

That from this Castles tatter'd Battlements

Our faire Appointments may be well perus'd.

Me thinkes King Richard and my selfe should meet

With no lesse terror then the Elements

Of Fire and Water, when their thundring smoake

At meeting teares the cloudie Cheekes of Heauen:

Be he the fire, Ile be the yeelding Water;

The Rage be his, while on the Earth I raine

My Waters on the Earth, and not on him.

March on, and marke King Richard how he lookes.

Parle without, and answere within: then a Flourish. Enter on the Walls,

Richard, Carlile, Aumerle, Scroop, Salisbury.

See, see, King Richard doth himselfe appeare

As doth the blushing discontented Sunne,

From out the fierie Portall of the East,

When he perceiues the enuious Clouds are bent

To dimme his glory, and to staine the tract

Of his bright passage to the Occident

York. Yet lookes he like a King: behold his Eye

(As bright as is the Eagles) lightens forth

Controlling Maiestie: alack, alack, for woe,

That any harme should staine so faire a shew

Rich. Wee are amaz'd, and thus long haue we stood

To watch the fearefull bending of thy knee,

Because we thought our selfe thy lawfull King:

And if we be, how dare thy ioynts forget

To pay their awfull dutie to our presence?

If we be not, shew vs the Hand of God,

That hath dismiss'd vs from our Stewardship,

For well wee know, no Hand of Blood and Bone

Can gripe the sacred Handle of our Scepter,

Vnlesse he doe prophane, steale, or vsurpe.

And though you thinke, that all, as you haue done,

Haue torne their Soules, by turning them from vs,

And we are barren, and bereft of Friends:

Yet know, my Master, God Omnipotent,

Is mustring in his Clouds, on our behalfe,

Armies of Pestilence, and they shall strike

Your Children yet vnborne, and vnbegot,

That lift your Vassall Hands against my Head,

And threat the Glory of my precious Crowne.

Tell Bullingbrooke, for yond me thinkes he is,

That euery stride he makes vpon my Land,

Is dangerous Treason: He is come to ope

The purple Testament of bleeding Warre;

But ere the Crowne he lookes for, liue in peace,

Ten thousand bloody crownes of Mothers Sonnes

Shall ill become the flower of Englands face,

Change the complexion of her Maid-pale Peace

To Scarlet Indignation, and bedew
Her Pastors Grasse with faithfull English Blood
North. The King of Heauen forbid our Lord the King
Should so with ciuill and vnciuill Armes
Be rush'd vpon: Thy thrice-noble Cousin,
Harry Bullingbrooke, doth humbly kisse thy hand,
And by the Honorable Tombe he sweares,
That stands vpon your Royall Grandsires Bones,
And by the Royalties of both your Bloods,
(Currents that spring from one most gracious Head)
And by the buried Hand of Warlike Gaunt,
And by the Worth and Honor of himselfe,
Comprising all that may be sworne, or said,
His comming hither hath no further scope,
Then for his Lineall Royalties, and to begge
Infranchisement immediate on his knees:
Which on thy Royall partie graunted once,
His glittering Armes he will commend to Rust,
His barbed Steedes to Stables, and his heart
To faithfull seruice of your Maiestie:
This sweares he, as he is a Prince, is iust,
And as I am a Gentleman, I credit him
Rich. Northumberland, say thus: The King returnes,
His Noble Cousin is right welcome hither,
And all the number of his faire demands
Shall be accomplish'd without contradiction:
With all the gracious vtterance thou hast,

Speake to his gentle hearing kind commends.

We doe debase our selfe (Cousin) doe we not,

To looke so poorely, and to speake so faire?

Shall we call back Northumberland, and send

Defiance to the Traytor, and so die?

Aum. No, good my Lord, let's fight with gentle words,

Till time lend friends, and friends their helpeful Swords

Rich. Oh God, oh God, that ere this tongue of mine,

That layd the Sentence of dread Banishment

On yond prowd man, should take it off againe

With words of sooth: Oh that I were as great

As is my Griefe, or lesser then my Name,

Or that I could forget what I haue beene,

Or not remember what I must be now:

Swell'st thou prowd heart? Ile giue thee scope to beat,

Since Foes haue scope to beat both thee and me

Aum. Northumberland comes backe from Bullingbrooke

Rich. What must the King doe now? must he submit?

The King shall doe it: Must he be depos'd?

The King shall be contented: Must he loose

The Name of King? o' Gods Name let it goe.

Ile giue my Iewels for a sett of Beades,

My gorgeous Pallace, for a Hermitage,

My gay Apparrell, for an Almes-mans Gowne,

My figur'd Goblets, for a Dish of Wood,

My Scepter, for a Palmers walking Staffe,

My Subiects, for a payre of carued Saints,

And my large Kingdome, for a little Graue,

A little little Graue, an obscure Graue.

Or Ile be buryed in the Kings high-way,

Some way of common Trade, where Subiects feet

May howrely trample on their Soueraignes Head:

For on my heart they tread now, whilest I liue;

And buryed once, why not vpon my Head?

Aumerle, thou weep'st (my tender-hearted Cousin)

Wee'le make foule Weather with despised Teares:

Our sighes, and they, shall lodge the Summer Corne,

And make a Dearth in this reuolting Land.

Or shall we play the Wantons with our Woes,

And make some prettie Match, with shedding Teares?

As thus: to drop them still vpon one place,

Till they haue fretted vs a payre of Graues,

Within the Earth: and therein lay'd, there lyes

Two Kinsmen, digg'd their Graues with weeping Eyes?

Would not this ill, doe well? Well, well, I see

I talke but idly, and you mock at mee.

Most mightie Prince, my Lord Northumberland,

What sayes King Bullingbrooke? Will his Maiestie

Giue Richard leaue to liue, till Richard die?

You make a Legge, and Bullingbrooke sayes I

North. My Lord, in the base Court he doth attend

To speake with you, may it please you to come downe

Rich. Downe, downe I come, like glist'ring Phaeton,

Wanting the manage of vnruly Iades.

In the base Court? base Court, where Kings grow base,

To come at Traytors Calls, and doe them Grace.

In the base Court come down: down Court, down King,

For night-Owls shrike, where mou[n]ting Larks should sing

Bull. What sayes his Maiestie?

North. Sorrow, and griefe of heart

Makes him speake fondly, like a frantick man:

Yet he is come

Bull. Stand all apart,

And shew faire dutie to his Maiestie.

My gracious Lord

Rich. Faire Cousin,

You debase your Princely Knee,

To make the base Earth prowd with kissing it.

Me rather had, my Heart might feele your Loue,

Then my vnpleas'd Eye see your Courtesie.

Vp Cousin, vp, your Heart is vp, I know,

Thus high at least, although your Knee be low

Bull. My gracious Lord, I come but for mine owne

Rich. Your owne is yours, and I am yours, and all

Bull. So farre be mine, my most redoubted Lord,

As my true seruice shall deserue your loue

Rich. Well you deseru'd:

They well deserue to haue,

That know the strong'st, and surest way to get.

Vnckle giue me your Hand: nay, drie your Eyes,

Teares shew their Loue, but want their Remedies.

Cousin, I am too young to be your Father,

Though you are old enough to be my Heire.

What you will haue, Ile giue, and willing to,

For doe we must, what force will haue vs doe.

Set on towards London:

Cousin, is it so?

Bull. Yea, my good Lord

Rich. Then I must not say, no.

Flourish.

Exeunt.

Scena Quarta.

Enter the Queene, and two Ladies

Qu. What sport shall we deuise here in this Garden,

To driue away the heauie thought of Care?

La. Madame, wee'le play at Bowles

Qu. 'Twill make me thinke the World is full of Rubs,

And that my fortune runnes against the Byas

La. Madame, wee'le Dance

Qu. My Legges can keepe no measure in Delight,

When my poore Heart no measure keepes in Griefe.

Therefore no Dancing (Girle) some other sport

La. Madame, wee'le tell Tales

Qu. Of Sorrow, or of Griefe?

La. Of eyther, Madame

Qu. Of neyther, Girle.

For if of Ioy, being altogether wanting,

It doth remember me the more of Sorrow:

Or if of Griefe, being altogether had,

It addes more Sorrow to my want of Ioy:

For what I haue, I need not to repeat;

And what I want, it bootes not to complaine

La. Madame, Ile sing

Qu. 'Tis well that thou hast cause:

But thou should'st please me better, would'st thou weepe

La. I could weepe, Madame, would it doe you good

Qu. And I could sing, would weeping doe me good,

And neuer borrow any Teare of thee.

Enter a Gardiner, and two Seruants.

But stay, here comes the Gardiners,

Let's step into the shadow of these Trees.

My wretchednesse, vnto a Rowe of Pinnes,

They'le talke of State: for euery one doth so,

Against a Change; Woe is fore-runne with Woe

Gard. Goe binde thou vp yond dangling Apricocks,

Which like vnruly Children, make their Syre

Stoupe with oppression of their prodigall weight:

Giue some supportance to the bending twigges.

Goe thou, and like an Executioner

Cut off the heads of too fast growing sprayes,

That looke too loftie in our Common-wealth:

All must be euen, in our Gouernment.

You thus imploy'd, I will goe root away

The noysome Weedes, that without profit sucke

The Soyles fertilitie from wholesome flowers

Ser. Why should we, in the compasse of a Pale,

Keepe Law and Forme, and due Proportion,

Shewing as in a Modell our firme Estate?

When our Sea-walled Garden, the whole Land,

Is full of Weedes, her fairest Flowers choakt vp,

Her Fruit-trees all vnpruin'd, her Hedges ruin'd,

Her Knots disorder'd, and her wholesome Hearbes

Swarming with Caterpillers

Gard. Hold thy peace.

He that hath suffer'd this disorder'd Spring,

Hath now himselfe met with the Fall of Leafe.

The Weeds that his broad-spreading Leaues did shelter,

That seem'd, in eating him, to hold him vp,

Are pull'd vp, Root and all, by Bullingbrooke:

I meane, the Earle of Wiltshire, Bushie, Greene

Ser. What are they dead?

Gard. They are,

And Bullingbrooke hath seiz'd the wastefull King.

Oh, what pitty is it, that he had not so trim'd

And drest his Land, as we this Garden, at time of yeare,

And wound the Barke, the skin of our Fruit-trees,

Least being ouer-proud with Sap and Blood,

With too much riches it confound it selfe?

Had he done so, to great and growing men,

They might haue liu'd to beare, and he to taste

Their fruites of dutie. Superfluous branches

We lop away, that bearing boughes may liue:

Had he done so, himselfe had borne the Crowne,

Which waste and idle houres, hath quite thrown downe

Ser. What thinke you the King shall be depos'd?

Gar. Deprest he is already, and depos'd

'Tis doubted he will be. Letters came last night

To a deere Friend of the Duke of Yorkes,

That tell blacke tydings

Qu. Oh I am prest to death through want of speaking:

Thou old Adams likenesse, set to dresse this Garden:

How dares thy harsh rude tongue sound this vnpleasing newes

What Eue? what Serpent hath suggested thee,

To make a second fall of cursed man?

Why do'st thou say, King Richard is depos'd,

Dar'st thou, thou little better thing then earth,

Diuine his downfall? Say, where, when, and how

Cam'st thou by this ill-tydings? Speake thou wretch

Gard. Pardon me Madam. Little ioy haue I

To breath these newes; yet what I say, is true;

King Richard, he is in the mighty hold

Of Bullingbrooke, their Fortunes both are weigh'd:

In your Lords Scale, is nothing but himselfe,

And some few Vanities, that make him light:

But in the Ballance of great Bullingbrooke,

Besides himselfe, are all the English Peeres,

And with that oddes he weighes King Richard downe.

Poste you to London, and you'l finde it so,

I speake no more, then euery one doth know

Qu. Nimble mischance, that art so light of foote,

Doth not thy Embassage belong to me?

And am I last that knowes it? Oh thou think'st

To serue me last, that I may longest keepe

Thy sorrow in my breast. Come Ladies goe,

To meet at London, Londons King in woe.

What was I borne to this: that my sad looke,

Should grace the Triumph of great Bullingbrooke.

Gard'ner, for telling me this newes of woe,

I would the Plants thou graft'st, may neuer grow.

Enter.

G. Poore Queen, so that thy State might be no worse,

I would my skill were subiect to thy curse:

Heere did she drop a teare, heere in this place

Ile set a Banke of Rew, sowre Herbe of Grace:

Rue, eu'n for ruth, heere shortly shall be seene,

In the remembrance of a Weeping Queene.

Enter.

Actus Quartus.

Scoena Prima.

Enter as to the Parliament, Bullingbrooke, Aumerle,

Northumberland,

Percie, FitzWater, Surrey, Carlile, Abbot of Westminster. Herauld,

Officers, and Bagot.

Bullingbrooke. Call forth Bagot.

Now Bagot, freely speake thy minde,

What thou do'st know of Noble Glousters death:

Who wrought it with the King, and who perform'd

The bloody Office of his Timelesse end

Bag. Then set before my face, the Lord Aumerle

Bul. Cosin, stand forth, and looke vpon that man

Bag. My Lord Aumerle, I know your daring tongue

Scornes to vnsay, what it hath once deliuer'd.

In that dead time, when Glousters death was plotted,

I heard you say, Is not my arme of length,

That reacheth from the restfull English Court

As farre as Callis, to my Vnkles head.

Amongst much other talke, that very time,

I heard you say, that you had rather refuse

The offer of an hundred thousand Crownes,

Then Bullingbrookes returne to England; adding withall,

How blest this Land would be, in this your Cosins death

Aum. Princes, and Noble Lords:

What answer shall I make to this base man?

Shall I so much dishonor my faire Starres,

On equall termes to giue him chasticement?

Either I must, or haue mine honor soyl'd

With th' Attaindor of his sland'rous Lippes.

There is my Gage, the manuall Seale of death

That markes thee out for Hell. Thou lyest,

And will maintaine what thou hast said, is false,

In thy heart blood, though being all too base

To staine the temper of my Knightly sword

Bul. Bagot forbeare, thou shalt not take it vp

Aum. Excepting one, I would he were the best

In all this presence, that hath mou'd me so

Fitz. If that thy valour stand on sympathize:

There is my Gage, Aumerle, in Gage to thine:

By that faire Sunne, that shewes me where thou stand'st,

I heard thee say (and vauntingly thou spak'st it)

That thou wer't cause of Noble Glousters death.

If thou deniest it, twenty times thou lyest,

And I will turne thy falshood to thy hart,

Where it was forged with my Rapiers point

Aum. Thou dar'st not (Coward) liue to see the day

Fitz. Now by my Soule, I would it were this houre

Aum. Fitzwater thou art damn'd to hell for this

Per. Aumerle, thou lye'st: his Honor is as true

In this Appeale, as thou art all vniust:

And that thou art so, there I throw my Gage

To proue it on thee, to th' extreamest point

Of mortall breathing. Seize it, if thou dar'st

Aum. And if I do not, may my hands rot off,

And neuer brandish more reuengefull Steele,

Ouer the glittering Helmet of my Foe

Surrey. My Lord Fitzwater:

I do remember well, the very time

Aumerle, and you did talke

Fitz. My Lord,

'Tis very true: You were in presence then,

And you can witnesse with me, this is true

Surrey. As false, by heauen,

As Heauen it selfe is true

Fitz. Surrey, thou Lyest

Surrey. Dishonourable Boy;

That Lye, shall lie so heauy on my Sword,

That it shall render Vengeance, and Reuenge,

Till thou the Lye-giuer, and that Lye, doe lye

In earth as quiet, as thy Fathers Scull.

In proofe whereof, there is mine Honors pawne,

Engage it to the Triall, if thou dar'st

Fitzw. How fondly do'st thou spurre a forward Horse?

If I dare eate, or drinke, or breathe, or liue,

I dare meete Surrey in a Wildernesse,

And spit vpon him, whilest I say he Lyes,

And Lyes, and Lyes: there is my Bond of Faith,

To tye thee to my strong Correction.

As I intend to thriue in this new World,

Aumerle is guiltie of my true Appeale.

Besides, I heard the banish'd Norfolke say,

That thou Aumerle didst send two of thy men,

To execute the Noble Duke at Callis

Aum. Some honest Christian trust me with a Gage,

That Norfolke lyes: here doe I throw downe this,

If he may be repeal'd, to trie his Honor

Bull. These differences shall all rest vnder Gage,

Till Norfolke be repeal'd: repeal'd he shall be;

And (though mine Enemie) restor'd againe
To all his Lands and Seignories: when hee's return'd,
Against Aumerle we will enforce his Tryall

Carl. That honorable day shall ne're be seene.
Many a time hath banish'd Norfolke fought
For Iesu Christ, in glorious Christian field
Streaming the Ensigne of the Christian Crosse,
Against black Pagans, Turkes, and Saracens:
And toyl'd with workes of Warre, retyr'd himselfe
To Italy, and there at Venice gaue
His Body to that pleasant Countries Earth,
And his pure Soule vnto his Captaine Christ,
Vnder whose Colours he had fought so long

Bull. Why Bishop, is Norfolke dead?

Carl. As sure as I liue, my Lord

Bull. Sweet peace conduct his sweet Soule
To the Bosome of good old Abraham.
Lords Appealants, your differe[n]ces shal all rest vnder gage,
Till we assigne you to your dayes of Tryall.

Enter Yorke.

Yorke. Great Duke of Lancaster, I come to thee
From plume-pluckt Richard, who with willing Soule
Adopts thee Heire, and his high Scepter yeelds
To the possession of thy Royall Hand.
Ascend his Throne, descending now from him,
And long liue Henry, of that Name the Fourth

Bull. In Gods Name, Ile ascend the Regall Throne

Carl. Mary, Heauen forbid.

Worst in this Royall Presence may I speake,

Yet best beseeming me to speake the truth.

Would God, that any in this Noble Presence

Were enough Noble, to be vpright Iudge

Of Noble Richard: then true Noblenesse would

Learne him forbearance from so foule a Wrong.

What Subiect can giue Sentence on his King?

And who sits here, that is not Richards Subiect?

Theeues are not iudg'd, but they are by to heare,

Although apparant guilt be seene in them:

And shall the figure of Gods Maiestie,

His Captaine, Steward, Deputie elect,

Anoynted, Crown'd, planted many yeeres,

Be iudg'd by subiect, and inferior breathe,

And he himselfe not present? Oh, forbid it, God,

That in a Christian Climate, Soules refin'de

Should shew so heynous, black, obscene a deed.

I speake to Subiects, and a Subiect speakes,

Stirr'd vp by Heauen, thus boldly for his King

My Lord of Hereford here, whom you call King,

Is a foule Traytor to prowd Herefords King.

And if you Crowne him, let me prophecie,

The blood of English shall manure the ground,

And future Ages groane for his foule Act.

Peace shall goe sleepe with Turkes and Infidels,

And in this Seat of Peace, tumultuous Warres

Shall Kinne with Kinne, and Kinde with Kinde confound.

Disorder, Horror, Feare, and Mutinie

Shall here inhabite, and this Land be call'd

The field of Golgotha, and dead mens Sculls.

Oh, if you reare this House, against this House

It will the wofullest Diuision proue,

That euer fell vpon this cursed Earth.

Preuent it, resist it, and let it not be so,

Least Child, Childs Children cry against you, Woe

North. Well haue you argu'd Sir: and for your paines,

Of Capitall Treason we arrest you here.

My Lord of Westminster, be it your charge,

To keepe him safely, till his day of Tryall.

May it please you, Lords, to grant the Commons Suit?

Bull. Fetch hither Richard, that in common view

He may surrender: so we shall proceede

Without suspition

Yorke. I will be his Conduct.

Enter.

Bull. Lords, you that here are vnder our Arrest,

Procure your Sureties for your Dayes of Answer:

Little are we beholding to your Loue,

And little look'd for at your helping Hands.

Enter Richard and Yorke.

Rich. Alack, why am I sent for to a King,

Before I haue shooke off the Regall thoughts

Wherewith I reign'd? I hardly yet haue learn'd

To insinuate, flatter, bowe, and bend my Knee.
Giue Sorrow leaue a while, to tuture me
To this submission. Yet I well remember
The fauors of these men: were they not mine?
Did they not sometime cry, All hayle to me?
So Iudas did to Christ: but he in twelue,
Found truth in all, but one; I, in twelue thousand, none.
God saue the King: will no man say, Amen?
Am I both Priest, and Clarke? well then, Amen.
God saue the King, although I be not hee:
And yet Amen, if Heauen doe thinke him mee.
To doe what seruice, am I sent for hither?
Yorke. To doe that office of thine owne good will,
Which tyred Maiestie did make thee offer:
The Resignation of thy State and Crowne
To Henry Bullingbrooke
Rich. Giue me the Crown. Here Cousin, seize y Crown:
Here Cousin, on this side my Hand, on that side thine.
Now is this Golden Crowne like a deepe Well,
That owes two Buckets, filling one another,
The emptier euer dancing in the ayre,
The other downe, vnseene, and full of Water:
That Bucket downe, and full of Teares am I,
Drinking my Griefes, whil'st you mount vp on high
Bull. I thought you had been willing to resigne
Rich. My Crowne I am, but still my Griefes are mine:
You may my Glories and my State depose,

But not my Griefes; still am I King of those

Bull. Part of your Cares you giue me with your Crowne

Rich. Your Cares set vp, do not pluck my Cares downe.

My Care, is losse of Care, by old Care done,

Your Care, is gaine of Care, by new Care wonne:

The Cares I giue, I haue, though giuen away,

They 'tend the Crowne, yet still with me they stay:

Bull. Are you contented to resigne the Crowne?

Rich. I, no; no, I: for I must nothing bee:

Therefore no, no, for I resigne to thee.

Now, marke me how I will vndoe my selfe.

I giue this heauie Weight from off my Head,

And this vnwieldie Scepter from my Hand,

The pride of Kingly sway from out my Heart.

With mine owne Teares I wash away my Balme,

With mine owne Hands I giue away my Crowne,

With mine owne Tongue denie my Sacred State,

With mine owne Breath release all dutious Oathes;

All Pompe and Maiestie I doe forsweare:

My Manors, Rents, Reuenues, I forgoe;

My Acts, Decrees, and Statutes I denie:

God pardon all Oathes that are broke to mee,

God keepe all Vowes vnbroke are made to thee.

Make me that nothing haue, with nothing grieu'd,

And thou with all pleas'd, that hast all atchieu'd.

Long may'st thou liue in Richards Seat to sit,

And soone lye Richard in an Earthie Pit.

God saue King Henry, vn-King'd Richard sayes,

And send him many yeeres of Sunne-shine dayes.

What more remaines?

North. No more: but that you reade

These Accusations, and these grieuous Crymes,

Committed by your Person, and your followers,

Against the State, and Profit of this Land:

That by confessing them, the Soules of men

May deeme, that you are worthily depos'd

Rich. Must I doe so? and must I rauell out

My weau'd-vp follyes? Gentle Northumberland,

If thy Offences were vpon Record,

Would it not shame thee, in so faire a troupe,

To reade a Lecture of them? If thou would'st,

There should'st thou finde one heynous Article,

Contayning the deposing of a King,

And cracking the strong Warrant of an Oath,

Mark'd with a Blot, damn'd in the Booke of Heauen.

Nay, all of you, that stand and looke vpon me,

Whil'st that my wretchednesse doth bait my selfe,

Though some of you, with Pilate, wash your hands,

Shewing an outward pittie: yet you Pilates

Haue here deliuer'd me to my sowre Crosse,

And Water cannot wash away your sinne

North. My Lord dispatch, reade o're these Articles

Rich. Mine Eyes are full of Teares, I cannot see:

And yet salt-Water blindes them not so much,

But they can see a sort of Traytors here.

Nay, if I turne mine Eyes vpon my selfe,

I finde my selfe a Traytor with the rest:

For I haue giuen here my Soules consent,

T' vndeck the pompous Body of a King;

Made Glory base; a Soueraigntie, a Slaue;

Prowd Maiestie, a Subiect; State, a Pesant

North. My Lord

Rich. No Lord of thine, thou haught-insulting man;

No, nor no mans Lord: I haue no Name, no Title;

No, not that Name was giuen me at the Font,

But 'tis vsurpt: alack the heauie day,

That I haue worne so many Winters out,

And know not now, what Name to call my selfe.

Oh, that I were a Mockerie, King of Snow,

Standing before the Sunne of Bullingbrooke,

To melt my selfe away in Water-drops.

Good King, great King, and yet not greatly good,

And if my word be Sterling yet in England,

Let it command a Mirror hither straight,

That it may shew me what a Face I haue,

Since it is Bankrupt of his Maiestie

Bull. Goe some of you, and fetch a Looking-Glasse

North. Read o're this Paper, while y Glasse doth come

Rich. Fiend, thou torments me, ere I come to Hell

Bull. Vrge it no more, my Lord Northumberland

North. The Commons will not then be satisfy'd

Rich. They shall be satisfy'd: Ile reade enough,

When I doe see the very Booke indeede,

Where all my sinnes are writ, and that's my selfe.

Enter one with a Glasse.

Giue me that Glasse, and therein will I reade.

No deeper wrinckles yet? hath Sorrow strucke

So many Blowes vpon this Face of mine,

And made no deeper Wounds? Oh flatt'ring Glasse,

Like to my followers in prosperitie,

Thou do'st beguile me. Was this Face, the Face

That euery day, vnder his House-hold Roofe,

Did keepe ten thousand men? Was this the Face,

That like the Sunne, did make beholders winke?

Is this the Face, which fac'd so many follyes,

That was at last out-fac'd by Bullingbrooke?

A brittle Glory shineth in this Face,

As brittle as the Glory, is the Face,

For there it is, crackt in an hundred shiuers.

Marke silent King, the Morall of this sport,

How soone my Sorrow hath destroy'd my Face

Bull. The shadow of your Sorrow hath destroy'd

The shadow of your Face

Rich. Say that againe.

The shadow of my Sorrow: ha, let's see,

'Tis very true, my Griefe lyes all within,

And these externall manner of Laments,

Are meerely shadowes, to the vnseene Griefe,

That swells with silence in the tortur'd Soule.
There lyes the substance: and I thanke thee King
For thy great bountie, that not onely giu'st
Me cause to wayle, but teachest me the way
How to lament the cause. Ile begge one Boone,
And then be gone, and trouble you no more.
Shall I obtaine it?
Bull. Name it, faire Cousin
Rich. Faire Cousin? I am greater then a King:
For when I was a King, my flatterers
Were then but subiects; being now a subiect,
I haue a King here to my flatterer:
Being so great, I haue no neede to begge
Bull. Yet aske
Rich. And shall I haue?
Bull. You shall
Rich. Then giue me leaue to goe
Bull. Whither?
Rich. Whither you will, so I were from your sights
Bull. Goe some of you, conuey him to the Tower
Rich. Oh good: conuey: Conueyers are you all,
That rise thus nimbly by a true Kings fall
Bull. On Wednesday next, we solemnly set downe
Our Coronation: Lords, prepare your selues.
   Exeunt.
Abbot. A wofull Pageant haue we here beheld
Carl. The Woes to come, the Children yet vnborne,

Shall feele this day as sharpe to them as Thorne

Aum. You holy Clergie-men, is there no Plot

To rid the Realme of this pernicious Blot

Abbot. Before I freely speake my minde herein,

You shall not onely take the Sacrament,

To bury mine intents, but also to effect

What euer I shall happen to deuise.

I see your Browes are full of Discontent,

Your Heart of Sorrow, and your Eyes of Teares.

Come home with me to Supper, Ile lay a Plot

Shall shew vs all a merry day.

    Exeunt.

Actus Quintus.

Scena Prima.

    Enter Queene, and Ladies.

Qu. This way the King will come: this is the way

To Iulius Cæsars ill-erected Tower:

To whose flint Bosome, my condemned Lord

Is doom'd a Prisoner, by prowd Bullingbrooke.

Here let vs rest, if this rebellious Earth

Haue any resting for her true Kings Queene.

    Enter Richard, and Guard.

But soft, but see, or rather doe not see,

My faire Rose wither: yet looke vp; behold,

That you in pittie may dissolue to dew,

And wash him fresh againe with true-loue Teares.

Ah thou, the Modell where old Troy did stand,
Thou Mappe of Honor, thou King Richards Tombe,
And not King Richard: thou most beauteous Inne,
Why should hard-fauor'd Griefe be lodg'd in thee,
When Triumph is become an Ale-house Guest
  Rich. Ioyne not with griefe, faire Woman, do not so,
To make my end too sudden: learne good Soule,
To thinke our former State a happie Dreame,
From which awak'd, the truth of what we are,
Shewes vs but this. I am sworne Brother (Sweet)
To grim Necessitie; and hee and I
Will keepe a League till Death. High thee to France,
And Cloyster thee in some Religious House:
Our holy liues must winne a new Worlds Crowne,
Which our prophane houres here haue stricken downe
  Qu. What, is my Richard both in shape and minde
Transform'd, and weaken'd? Hath Bullingbrooke
Depos'd thine Intellect? hath he beene in thy Heart?
The Lyon dying, thrusteth forth his Paw,
And wounds the Earth, if nothing else, with rage
To be o're-powr'd: and wilt thou, Pupill-like,
Take thy Correction mildly, kisse the Rodde,
And fawne on Rage with base Humilitie,
Which art a Lyon, and a King of Beasts?
  Rich. A King of Beasts indeed: if aught but Beasts,
I had beene still a happy King of Men.
Good (sometime Queene) prepare thee hence for France:

Thinke I am dead, and that euen here thou tak'st,

As from my Death-bed, my last liuing leaue.

In Winters tedious Nights sit by the fire

With good old folkes, and let them tell thee Tales

Of wofull Ages, long agoe betide:

And ere thou bid good-night, to quit their griefe,

Tell thou the lamentable fall of me,

And send the hearers weeping to their Beds:

For why? the sencelesse Brands will sympathize

The heauie accent of thy mouing Tongue,

And in compassion, weepe the fire out:

And some will mourne in ashes, some coale-black,

For the deposing of a rightfull King.

 Enter Northumberland.

North. My Lord, the mind of Bullingbrooke is chang'd.

You must to Pomfret, not vnto the Tower.

And Madame, there is order ta'ne for you:

With all swift speed, you must away to France

Rich. Northumberland, thou Ladder wherewithall

The mounting Bullingbrooke ascends my Throne,

The time shall not be many houres of age,

More then it is, ere foule sinne, gathering head,

Shall breake into corruption: thou shalt thinke,

Though he diuide the Realme, and giue thee halfe,

It is too little, helping him to all:

He shall thinke, that thou which know'st the way

To plant vnrightfull Kings, wilt know againe,

Being ne're so little vrg'd another way,

To pluck him headlong from the vsurped Throne.

The Loue of wicked friends conuerts to Feare;

That Feare, to Hate; and Hate turnes one, or both,

To worthie Danger, and deserued Death

North. My guilt be on my Head, and there an end:

Take leaue, and part, for you must part forthwith

Rich. Doubly diuorc'd? (bad men) ye violate

A two-fold Marriage; 'twixt my Crowne, and me.

And then betwixt me, and my marryed Wife.

Let me vn-kisse the Oath 'twixt thee, and me;

And yet not so, for with a Kisse 'twas made.

Part vs, Northumberland: I, towards the North,

Where shiuering Cold and Sicknesse pines the Clyme:

My Queene to France: from whence, set forth in pompe,

She came adorned hither like sweet May;

Sent back like Hollowmas, or short'st of day

Qu. And must we be diuided? must we part?

Rich. I, hand from hand (my Loue) and heart fro[m] heart

Qu. Banish vs both, and send the King with me

North. That were some Loue, but little Pollicy

Qu. Then whither he goes, thither let me goe

Rich. So two together weeping, make one Woe.

Weepe thou for me in France; I, for thee heere:

Better farre off, then neere, be ne're the neere.

Goe, count thy Way with Sighes; I, mine with Groanes

Qu. So longest Way shall haue the longest Moanes

Rich. Twice for one step Ile groane, y Way being short,

And peece the Way out with a heauie heart.

Come, come, in wooing Sorrow let's be briefe,

Since wedding it, there is such length in Griefe:

One Kisse shall stop our mouthes, and dumbely part;

Thus giue I mine, and thus take I thy heart

Qu. Giue me mine owne againe: 'twere no good part,

To take on me to keepe, and kill thy heart.

So, now I haue mine owne againe, be gone,

That I may striue to kill it with a groane

Rich. We make Woe wanton with this fond delay:

Once more adieu; the rest, let Sorrow say.

    Exeunt.

Scena Secunda.

    Enter Yorke, and his Duchesse.

Duch. My Lord, you told me you would tell the rest,

When weeping made you breake the story off,

Of our two Cousins comming into London

Yorke. Where did I leaue?

Duch. At that sad stoppe, my Lord,

Where rude mis-gouern'd hands, from Windowes tops,

Threw dust and rubbish on King Richards head

Yorke. Then, as I said, the Duke, great Bullingbrooke,

Mounted vpon a hot and fierie Steed,

Which his aspiring Rider seem'd to know,

With slow, but stately pace, kept on his course:

While all tongues cride, God saue thee Bullingbrooke.

You would haue thought the very windowes spake,

So many greedy lookes of yong and old,

Through Casements darted their desiring eyes

Vpon his visage: and that all the walles,

With painted Imagery had said at once,

Iesu preserue thee, welcom Bullingbrooke.

Whil'st he, from one side to the other turning,

Bare-headed, lower then his proud Steeds necke,

Bespake them thus: I thanke you Countrimen:

And thus still doing, thus he past along

Dutch. Alas poore Richard, where rides he the whilst?

Yorke. As in a Theater, the eyes of men

After a well grac'd Actor leaues the Stage,

Are idlely bent on him that enters next,

Thinking his prattle to be tedious:

Euen so, or with much more contempt, mens eyes

Did scowle on Richard: no man cride, God saue him:

No ioyfull tongue gaue him his welcome home,

But dust was throwne vpon his Sacred head,

Which with such gentle sorrow he shooke off,

His face still combating with teares and smiles

(The badges of his greefe and patience)

That had not God (for some strong purpose) steel'd

The hearts of men, they must perforce haue melted,

And Barbarisme it selfe haue pittied him.

But heauen hath a hand in these euents,

To whose high will we bound our calme contents.

To Bullingbrooke, are we sworne Subiects now,

Whose State, and Honor, I for aye allow.

    Enter Aumerle

Dut. Heere comes my sonne Aumerle

Yor. Aumerle that was,

But that is lost, for being Richards Friend.

And Madam, you must call him Rutland now:

I am in Parliament pledge for his truth,

And lasting fealtie to the new-made King

Dut. Welcome my sonne: who are the Violets now,

That strew the greene lap of the new-come Spring?

Aum. Madam, I know not, nor I greatly care not,

God knowes, I had as liefe be none, as one

Yorke. Well, beare you well in this new-spring of time

Least you be cropt before you come to prime.

What newes from Oxford? Hold those Iusts & Triumphs?

Aum. For ought I know my Lord, they do

Yorke. You will be there I know

Aum. If God preuent not, I purpose so

Yor. What Seale is that that hangs without thy bosom?

Yea, look'st thou pale? Let me see the Writing

Aum. My Lord, 'tis nothing

Yorke. No matter then who sees it,

I will be satisfied, let me see the Writing

Aum. I do beseech your Grace to pardon me,

It is a matter of small consequence,

Which for some reasons I would not haue seene

Yorke. Which for some reasons sir, I meane to see:

I feare, I feare

Dut. What should you feare?

'Tis nothing but some bond, that he is enter'd into

For gay apparrell, against the Triumph

Yorke. Bound to himselfe? What doth he with a Bond

That he is bound to? Wife, thou art a foole.

Boy, let me see the Writing

Aum. I do beseech you pardon me, I may not shew it

Yor. I will be satisfied: let me see it I say.

Snatches it

Treason, foule Treason, Villaine, Traitor, Slaue

Dut. What's the matter, my Lord?

Yorke. Hoa, who's within there? Saddle my horse.

Heauen for his mercy: what treachery is heere?

Dut. Why, what is't my Lord?

Yorke. Giue me my boots, I say: Saddle my horse:

Now by my Honor, my life, my troth,

I will appeach the Villaine

Dut. What is the matter?

Yorke. Peace foolish Woman

Dut. I will not peace. What is the matter Sonne?

Aum. Good Mother be content, it is no more

Then my poore life must answer

Dut. Thy life answer?

  Enter Seruant with Boots.

Yor. Bring me my Boots, I will vnto the King

Dut. Strike him Aumerle. Poore boy, y art amaz'd,

Hence Villaine, neuer more come in my sight

Yor. Giue me my Boots, I say

Dut. Why Yorke, what wilt thou do?

Wilt thou not hide the Trespasse of thine owne?

Haue we more Sonnes? Or are we like to haue?

Is not my teeming date drunke vp with time?

And wilt thou plucke my faire Sonne from mine Age,

And rob me of a happy Mothers name?

Is he not like thee? Is he not thine owne?

Yor. Thou fond mad woman:

Wilt thou conceale this darke Conspiracy?

A dozen of them heere haue tane the Sacrament,

And interchangeably set downe their hands

To kill the King at Oxford

Dut. He shall be none:

Wee'l keepe him heere: then what is that to him?

Yor. Away fond woman: were hee twenty times my

Son, I would appeach him

Dut. Hadst thou groan'd for him as I haue done,

Thou wouldest be more pittifull:

But now I know thy minde; thou do'st suspect

That I haue bene disloyall to thy bed,

And that he is a Bastard, not thy Sonne:

Sweet Yorke, sweet husband, be not of that minde:

He is as like thee, as a man may bee,

Not like to me, nor any of my Kin,

And yet I loue him

Yorke. Make way, vnruly Woman.

Exit

Dut. After Aumerle. Mount thee vpon his horse,

Spurre post, and get before him to the King,

And begge thy pardon, ere he do accuse thee,

Ile not be long behind: though I be old,

I doubt not but to ride as fast as Yorke:

And neuer will I rise vp from the ground,

Till Bullingbrooke haue pardon'd thee: Away be gone.

Exit

Scena Tertia.

Enter Bullingbrooke, Percie, and other Lords.
Bul. Can no man tell of my vnthriftie Sonne?
'Tis full three monthes since I did see him last.
If any plague hang ouer vs, 'tis he,
I would to heauen (my Lords) he might be found:
Enquire at London, 'mongst the Tauernes there:
For there (they say) he dayly doth frequent,
With vnrestrained loose Companions,
Euen such (they say) as stand in narrow Lanes,
And rob our Watch, and beate our passengers,
Which he, yong wanton, and effeminate Boy
Takes on the point of Honor, to support
So dissolute a crew

Per. My Lord, some two dayes since I saw the Prince,

And told him of these Triumphes held at Oxford

Bul. And what said the Gallant?

Per. His answer was: he would vnto the Stewes,

And from the common'st creature plucke a Gloue

And weare it as a fauour, and with that

He would vnhorse the lustiest Challenger

Bul. As dissolute as desp'rate, yet through both,

I see some sparkes of better hope: which elder dayes

May happily bring forth. But who comes heere?

    Enter Aumerle.

Aum. Where is the King?

Bul. What meanes our Cosin, that hee stares

And lookes so wildely?

Aum. God saue your Grace. I do beseech your Maiesty

To haue some conference with your Grace alone

Bul. Withdraw your selues, and leaue vs here alone:

What is the matter with our Cosin now?

Aum. For euer may my knees grow to the earth,

My tongue cleaue to my roofe within my mouth,

Vnlesse a Pardon, ere I rise, or speake

Bul. Intended, or committed was this fault?

If on the first, how heynous ere it bee,

To win thy after loue, I pardon thee

Aum. Then giue me leaue, that I may turne the key,

That no man enter, till my tale be done

Bul. Haue thy desire.

Yorke within.

Yor. My Liege beware, looke to thy selfe,
Thou hast a Traitor in thy presence there
Bul. Villaine, Ile make thee safe
Aum. Stay thy reuengefull hand, thou hast no cause
to feare
Yorke. Open the doore, secure foole-hardy King:
Shall I for loue speake treason to thy face?
Open the doore, or I will breake it open.

    Enter Yorke.

Bul. What is the matter (Vnkle) speak, recouer breath,
Tell vs how neere is danger,
That we may arme vs to encounter it
Yor. Peruse this writing heere, and thou shalt know
The reason that my haste forbids me show
Aum. Remember as thou read'st, thy promise past:
I do repent me, reade not my name there,
My heart is not confederate with my hand
Yor. It was (villaine) ere thy hand did set it downe.
I tore it from the Traitors bosome, King.
Feare, and not Loue, begets his penitence;
Forget to pitty him, least thy pitty proue
A Serpent, that will sting thee to the heart
Bul. Oh heinous, strong, and bold Conspiracie,
O loyall Father of a treacherous Sonne:
Thou sheere, immaculate, and siluer fountaine,
From whence this streame, through muddy passages

Hath had his current, and defil'd himselfe.
Thy ouerflow of good, conuerts to bad,
And thy abundant goodnesse shall excuse
This deadly blot, in thy digressing sonne
Yorke. So shall my Vertue be his Vices bawd,
And he shall spend mine Honour, with his Shame;
As thriftlesse Sonnes, their scraping Fathers Gold.
Mine honor liues, when his dishonor dies,
Or my sham'd life, in his dishonor lies:
Thou kill'st me in his life, giuing him breath,
The Traitor liues, the true man's put to death.
Dutchesse within.
Dut. What hoa (my Liege) for heauens sake let me in
Bul. What shrill-voic'd Suppliant, makes this eager cry?
Dut. A woman, and thine Aunt (great King) 'tis I.
Speake with me, pitty me, open the dore,
A Begger begs, that neuer begg'd before
Bul. Our Scene is alter'd from a serious thing,
And now chang'd to the Begger, and the King.
My dangerous Cosin, let your Mother in,
I know she's come, to pray for your foule sin
Yorke. If thou do pardon, whosoeuer pray,
More sinnes for this forgiuenesse, prosper may.
This fester'd ioynt cut off, the rest rests sound,
This let alone, will all the rest confound.

    Enter Dutchesse.

Dut. O King, beleeue not this hard-hearted man,

Loue, louing not it selfe, none other can

Yor. Thou franticke woman, what dost y make here,

Shall thy old dugges, once more a Traitor reare?

Dut. Sweet Yorke be patient, heare me gentle Liege

Bul. Rise vp good Aunt

Dut. Not yet, I thee beseech.

For euer will I kneele vpon my knees,

And neuer see day, that the happy sees,

Till thou giue ioy: vntill thou bid me ioy,

By pardoning Rutland, my transgressing Boy

Aum. Vnto my mothers prayres, I bend my knee

Yorke. Against them both, my true ioynts bended be

Dut. Pleades he in earnest? Looke vpon his Face,

His eyes do drop no teares: his prayres are in iest:

His words come from his mouth, ours from our brest.

He prayes but faintly, and would be denide,

We pray with heart, and soule, and all beside:

His weary ioynts would gladly rise, I know,

Our knees shall kneele, till to the ground they grow:

His prayers are full of false hypocrisie,

Ours of true zeale, and deepe integritie:

Our prayers do out-pray his, then let them haue

That mercy, which true prayers ought to haue

Bul. Good Aunt stand vp

Dut. Nay, do not say stand vp.

But Pardon first, and afterwards stand vp.

And if I were thy Nurse, thy tongue to teach,

Pardon should be the first word of thy speach.

I neuer long'd to heare a word till now:

Say Pardon (King,) let pitty teach thee how.

The word is short: but not so short as sweet,

No word like Pardon, for Kings mouth's so meet

Yorke. Speake it in French (King) say Pardon'ne moy

Dut. Dost thou teach pardon, Pardon to destroy?

Ah my sowre husband, my hard-hearted Lord,

That set's the word it selfe, against the word.

Speake Pardon, as 'tis currant in our Land,

The chopping French we do not vnderstand.

Thine eye begins to speake, set thy tongue there,

Or in thy pitteous heart, plant thou thine eare,

That hearing how our plaints and prayres do pearce,

Pitty may moue thee, Pardon to rehearse

Bul. Good Aunt, stand vp

Dut. I do not sue to stand,

Pardon is all the suite I haue in hand

Bul. I pardon him, as heauen shall pardon mee

Dut. O happy vantage of a kneeling knee?

Yet am I sicke for feare: Speake it againe,

Twice saying Pardon, doth not pardon twaine,

But makes one pardon strong

Bul. I pardon him with all my hart

Dut. A God on earth thou art

Bul. But for our trusty brother-in-Law, the Abbot,

With all the rest of that consorted crew,

Destruction straight shall dogge them at the heeles:

Good Vnckle helpe to order seuerall powres

To Oxford, or where ere these Traitors are:

They shall not liue within this world I sweare,

But I will haue them, if I once know where.

Vnckle farewell, and Cosin adieu:

Your mother well hath praid, and proue you true

Dut. Come my old son, I pray heauen make thee new.

> *Exeunt.*
> *Enter Exton and Seruants.*

Ext. Didst thou not marke the King what words hee spake?

Haue I no friend will rid me of this liuing feare:

Was it not so?

Ser. Those were his very words.

Ex.

Haue I no Friend? (quoth he:) he spake it twice,

And vrg'd it twice together, did he not?

Ser. He did.

Ex.

And speaking it, he wistly look'd on me,

As who should say, I would thou wer't the man

That would diuorce this terror from my heart,

Meaning the King at Pomfret: Come, let's goe;

I am the Kings Friend, and will rid his Foe.

> *Enter.*

Scena Quarta.

Enter Richard.

Rich. I haue bin studying, how to compare

This Prison where I liue, vnto the World:

And for because the world is populous,

And heere is not a Creature, but my selfe,

I cannot do it: yet Ile hammer't out.

My Braine, Ile proue the Female to my Soule,

My Soule, the Father: and these two beget

A generation of still breeding Thoughts;

And these same Thoughts, people this Little World

In humors, like the people of this world,

For no thought is contented. The better sort,

As thoughts of things Diuine, are intermixt

With scruples, and do set the Faith it selfe

Against the Faith: as thus: Come litle ones: & then again,

It is as hard to come, as for a Camell

To thred the posterne of a Needles eye.

Thoughts tending to Ambition, they do plot

Vnlikely wonders; how these vaine weake nailes

May teare a passage through the Flinty ribbes

Of this hard world, my ragged prison walles:

And for they cannot, dye in their owne pride.

Thoughts tending to Content, flatter themselues,

That they are not the first of Fortunes slaues,

Nor shall not be the last. Like silly Beggars,

Who sitting in the Stockes, refuge their shame

That many haue, and others must sit there;

And in this Thought, they finde a kind of ease,
Bearing their owne misfortune on the backe
Of such as haue before indur'd the like.
Thus play I in one Prison, many people,
And none contented. Sometimes am I King;
Then Treason makes me wish my selfe a Beggar,
And so I am. Then crushing penurie,
Perswades me, I was better when a King:
Then am I king'd againe: and by and by,
Thinke that I am vn-king'd by Bullingbrooke,
And straight am nothing. But what ere I am,
Musick
Nor I, nor any man, that but man is,
With nothing shall be pleas'd, till he be eas'd
With being nothing. Musicke do I heare?
Ha, ha? keepe time: How sowre sweet Musicke is,
When Time is broke, and no Proportion kept?
So is it in the Musicke of mens liues:
And heere haue I the daintinesse of eare,
To heare time broke in a disorder'd string:
But for the Concord of my State and Time,
Had not an eare to heare my true Time broke.
I wasted Time, and now doth Time waste me:
For now hath Time made me his numbring clocke;
My Thoughts, are minutes; and with Sighes they iarre,
Their watches on vnto mine eyes, the outward Watch,
Whereto my finger, like a Dialls point,

Is pointing still, in cleansing them from teares.
Now sir, the sound that tels what houre it is,
Are clamorous groanes, that strike vpon my heart,
Which is the bell: so Sighes, and Teares, and Grones,
Shew Minutes, Houres, and Times: but my Time
Runs poasting on, in Bullingbrookes proud ioy,
While I stand fooling heere, his iacke o'th' Clocke.
This Musicke mads me, let it sound no more,
For though it haue holpe madmen to their wits,
In me it seemes, it will make wise-men mad:
Yet blessing on his heart that giues it me;
For 'tis a signe of loue, and loue to Richard,
Is a strange Brooch, in this all-hating world.

    Enter Groome.

Groo. Haile Royall Prince
Rich. Thankes Noble Peere,
The cheapest of vs, is ten groates too deere.
What art thou? And how com'st thou hither?
Where no man euer comes, but that sad dogge
That brings me food, to make misfortune liue?
Groo. I was a poore Groome of thy Stable (King)
When thou wer't King: who trauelling towards Yorke,
With much adoo, at length haue gotten leaue
To looke vpon my (sometimes Royall) masters face.
O how it yern'd my heart, when I beheld
In London streets, that Coronation day,
When Bullingbrooke rode on Roane Barbary,

That horse, that thou so often hast bestrid,

That horse, that I so carefully haue drest

Rich. Rode he on Barbary? Tell me gentle Friend,

How went he vnder him?

Groo. So proudly, as if he had disdain'd the ground

Rich. So proud, that Bullingbrooke was on his backe;

That Iade hath eate bread from my Royall hand.

This hand hath made him proud with clapping him.

Would he not stumble? Would he not fall downe

(Since Pride must haue a fall) and breake the necke

Of that proud man, that did vsurpe his backe?

Forgiuenesse horse: Why do I raile on thee,

Since thou created to be aw'd by man

Was't borne to beare? I was not made a horse,

And yet I beare a burthen like an Asse,

Spur-gall'd, and tyrd by iauncing Bullingbrooke.

    Enter Keeper with a Dish.

Keep. Fellow, giue place, heere is no longer stay

Rich. If thou loue me, 'tis time thou wer't away

Groo. What my tongue dares not, that my heart shall say.

    Enter.

Keep. My Lord, wilt please you to fall too?

Rich. Taste of it first, as thou wer't wont to doo

Keep. My Lord I dare not: Sir Pierce of Exton,

Who lately came from th' King, commands the contrary

Rich. The diuell take Henrie of Lancaster, and thee;

Patience is stale, and I am weary of it

Keep. Helpe, helpe, helpe.

   Enter Exton and Seruants.

Ri. How now? what meanes Death in this rude assalt?

Villaine, thine owne hand yeelds thy deaths instrument,

Go thou and fill another roome in hell.

Exton strikes him downe.

That hand shall burne in neuer-quenching fire,

That staggers thus my person. Exton, thy fierce hand,

Hath with the Kings blood, stain'd the Kings own land.

Mount, mount my soule, thy seate is vp on high,

Whil'st my grosse flesh sinkes downward, heere to dye

Exton. As full of Valor, as of Royall blood,

Both haue I spilt: Oh would the deed were good.

For now the diuell, that told me I did well,

Sayes, that this deede is chronicled in hell.

This dead King to the liuing King Ile beare,

Take hence the rest, and giue them buriall heere.

   Enter.

Scena Quinta.

Flourish. Enter Bullingbrooke, Yorke, with other Lords & attendants.

Bul. Kinde Vnkle Yorke, the latest newes we heare,

Is that the Rebels haue consum'd with fire

Our Towne of Cicester in Gloucestershire,

But whether they be tane or slaine, we heare not.

   Enter Northumberland.

Welcome my Lord: What is the newes?

Nor. First to thy Sacred State, wish I all happinesse:

The next newes is, I haue to London sent

The heads of Salsbury, Spencer, Blunt, and Kent:

The manner of their taking may appeare

At large discoursed in this paper heere

Bul. We thank thee gentle Percy for thy paines,

And to thy worth will adde right worthy gaines.

Enter Fitzwaters.

Fitz. My Lord, I haue from Oxford sent to London,

The heads of Broccas, and Sir Bennet Seely,

Two of the dangerous consorted Traitors,

That sought at Oxford, thy dire ouerthrow

Bul. Thy paines Fitzwaters shall not be forgot,

Right Noble is thy merit, well I wot.

Enter Percy and Carlile.

Per. The grand Conspirator, Abbot of Westminster,

With clog of Conscience, and sowre Melancholly,

Hath yeelded vp his body to the graue:

But heere is Carlile, liuing to abide

Thy Kingly doome, and sentence of his pride

Bul. Carlile, this is your doome:

Choose out some secret place, some reuerend roome

More then thou hast, and with it ioy thy life:

So as thou liu'st in peace, dye free from strife:

For though mine enemy, thou hast euer beene,

High sparkes of Honor in thee haue I seene.

Enter Exton with a Coffin.

Exton. Great King, within this Coffin I present

Thy buried feare. Heerein all breathlesse lies

The mightiest of thy greatest enemies

Richard of Burdeaux, by me hither brought

Bul. Exton, I thanke thee not, for thou hast wrought

A deede of Slaughter, with thy fatall hand,

Vpon my head, and all this famous Land.

Ex.

From your owne mouth my Lord, did I this deed

Bul. They loue not poyson, that do poyson neede,

Nor do I thee: though I did wish him dead,

I hate the Murtherer, loue him murthered.

The guilt of conscience take thou for thy labour,

But neither my good word, nor Princely fauour.

With Caine go wander through the shade of night,

And neuer shew thy head by day, nor light.

Lords, I protest my soule is full of woe,

That blood should sprinkle me, to make me grow.

Come mourne with me, for that I do lament,

And put on sullen Blacke incontinent:

Ile make a voyage to the Holy-land,

To wash this blood off from my guilty hand.

March sadly after, grace my mourning heere,

In weeping after this vntimely Beere.

Exeunt.

FINIS. The life and death of King Richard the Second.

www.ingramcontent.com/pod-product-compliance
Lightning Source LLC
LaVergne TN
LVHW040107080526
838202LV00045B/3803